About Island Press

Since 1984, the nonprofit organization Island Press has been stimulating, shaping, and communicating ideas that are essential for solving environmental problems worldwide. With more than 1,000 titles in print and some 30 new releases each year, we are the nation's leading publisher on environmental issues. We identify innovative thinkers and emerging trends in the environmental field. We work with world-renowned experts and authors to develop cross-disciplinary solutions to environmental challenges.

Island Press designs and executes educational campaigns, in conjunction with our authors, to communicate their critical messages in print, in person, and online using the latest technologies, innovative programs, and the media. Our goal is to reach targeted audiences—scientists, policy makers, environmental advocates, urban planners, the media, and concerned citizens—with information that can be used to create the framework for long-term ecological health and human well-being.

Island Press gratefully acknowledges major support from The Bobolink Foundation, Caldera Foundation, The Curtis and Edith Munson Foundation, The Forrest C. and Frances H. Lattner Foundation, The JPB Foundation, The Kresge Foundation, The Summit Charitable Foundation, Inc., and many other generous organizations and individuals.

The opinions expressed in this book are those of the author(s) and do not necessarily reflect the views of our supporters.

Fixation

Fixation

HOW TO HAVE STUFF WITHOUT BREAKING THE PLANET

Sandra Goldmark

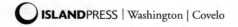

ISLANDPRESS | Washington | Covelo

This book was supported by a grant from Furthermore: a program of the J. M. Kaplan Fund.

Furthermore:
a program of the J.M.Kaplan Fund

Library of Congress Control Number: 2020939049

All Island Press books are printed on environmentally responsible materials.

Manufactured in the United States of America
10 9 8 7 6 5 4 3 2 1

Keywords: repair, fix, reuse, circular economy, sustainability, consumption, design, climate change, stuff, material culture, waste, theatre, scenery, swap, community, maintenance, innovation

For my family

Contents

Author's Note

I turned in the manuscript for this book in the first days of March 2020. I received a copyedited version back from the publisher a few weeks later, in early April. During that month, the coronavirus had spread across the globe. Every day, I watched the little red dots indicating virus hot spots on world maps expand, especially the ballooning circle that hovered over New York City. By the end of the month, my husband and I had both been infected with COVID-19, and very thankfully recovered. But in the meantime, the world had turned upside down.

As I got my energy back and dug into reviewing the copyedits, I had to ask what this new landscape meant for this book, and for what I had come to see as my work in the world. Did it still make sense to advocate for a healthy relationship with our stuff? Do the urgent needs of millions of unemployed people mean that we must return to "normal" at all costs, even if the pre-virus normal was deeply flawed? How do we think about climate change and consumption in the context of the pandemic?

As many have observed, climate change and the coronavirus have much in common: disproportionate impacts on the most vulnerable, a brutal uncovering of social inequity and flaws in our social safety nets, and the capacity to disrupt the flows of people, resources, food, and, yes, stuff around the world. The difference is speed. Climate change has been moving slowly, in the background, for years—and will continue to do so. Coronavirus came as a shock, thrusting all these questions, and more, abruptly into the foreground.

However, rather than seeing these crises as either-or, it's possible to perceive them as part of one process, operating at vastly different time scales: a reckoning that asks us to reexamine normal. As we rebuild after coronavirus, it's imperative that we rebuild sustainably and equitably. It's my hope that the simple steps offered in these pages will serve us as we move forward.

Pope Francis said of the coronavirus, "But let us not lose our memory once all this is past, let us not file it away and go back to where we were. This is the time to take the decisive step, to move from using and misusing nature to contemplating it."[1] The pages that follow are in large part a record of my learning to really see, or contemplate, the mundane objects all around me and to imagine a world where we don't simply use and misuse but begin to understand ourselves in relation to all that surrounds us. I hope that as we rebuild, we might, with what the pope calls "simple creativity," reimagine our relationship with our stuff, with the planet, and with one another.

May 7, 2020

INTRODUCTION:

Broken Sleep

Stuff is broken.

Our massive global system of consumption is broken—and it's breaking the planet. Our individual relationship with our own stuff is broken. And in each of our homes, some actual stuff is broken.

How do we fix it?

Maybe in your home you have a flickering lamp, a wobbly chair, a wimpy vacuum. Where do you go to get them fixed? It's a surprisingly difficult question, isn't it? Chances are your broken stuff languishes in your closet until some theoretical day when you can get around to dealing with it. It's frustrating, because you actually like your stuff. But it's just too inconvenient—and finally, you give up. And your broken lamp or chair or vacuum joins the 150 million tons of landfill we create every year in the United States. And your new lamp or vacuum contributes to global emissions, toxic working conditions, and even more waste—and the familiar, destructive cycle continues. It doesn't feel good.

This is the story of how I learned to feel good about having stuff. It took me more than seven years of repairing upwards of 2,500 broken objects to come up with a better, simpler way forward, both for individuals and for society. This is a story about finding easy steps toward a simpler, healthier, more sustainable relationship with our stuff—starting now.

The Toaster Oven

You are reading these words because my toaster broke. And my desk lamp. And the strap on my backpack. And my vacuum. This small tsunami of broken stuff occurred in 2013, when I was home on maternity leave with my husband, Michael, our four-year-old son, Luke, and newborn Eric.

It was a wonderful time to be home, to be a mother, and to feel the joy of being with my children. But as parents of new babies know, those precious early months are also a time of incredible upheaval, occasional irrationality, and dismal, fractured sleep. At night, when the baby needed to be nursed (or bounced on that infernal yoga ball, or cried until we carried him up and down the hall, or woke just to kick me awake and then drift into slumber himself), I had trouble falling back to sleep. I would lie in my bed, sometimes for hours, thinking about things.

I thought about small things: how much clutter seemed to be accumulating in our small New York apartment every Christmas and birthday that went by, not to mention all the baby gear. It piled up like a one-way flow behind a reservoir dam—lots and lots of new stuff in, and only a small trickle out. I thought about big things: the impact of manufacturing all that new, unneeded stuff on the deeply imperiled planet my young kids would grow up on. And sometimes I got stuck thinking about small things: the toaster and the vacuum and the rest of my little collection of broken objects just hanging around the house, collecting dust and unable to do their jobs. The vacuum manufacturer recommended visiting the nearest service center, in Hackensack, New Jersey. Needless to say (remember the newborn and the toddler), this was not likely to happen. Add to that the separate errands required for the backpack, the toaster, and the lamp, and the effort involved in simply maintaining the perfectly good things that I already had was beginning to feel insurmountable. Amazon beckoned. But I didn't want to get a new vacuum—I wanted the old one to work. And in the wilderness of fractured sleep that is newborn-dom, I tossed and turned, groping for a way forward.

I lay awake at night, yearning for rest, terrified about climate change, and thinking about my damn vacuum.

I began to connect the dots. I thought about how the vacuum, and desk lamp, and backpack, and toaster are part of a much bigger economic system of large-scale extraction of resources, poor design, rapid manufacture, global distribution, early obsolescence, and disposal. I thought about what it means to raise kids in a culture where we place almost no value on longevity, maintenance, durability—on care. Where many of the things we use are disposable. Where many of the things around us are toxic to the people who make them, the people who use them, and to the planet. Where many of us are disconnected from the people who make our things, and from our ability to make (or mend) our own things. And where we are extracting and using resources at an unsustainable rate to make things that are, often, just crap. I wondered, what does this mean for our bodies, our lives, our children—for the road we are hurtling down as a species? For the story we are living as thinking beings? And I thought: What might I—we—be able to do about it?

For starters, I imagined how nice it would be if it were possible, maybe even easy, to get things fixed again. The reality today here in the United States is that if you or I want a broken vacuum to work again, our options are very limited. Repair services are fewer and farther between, and many products are designed for quick replacement. Prices for new stuff are kept artificially low by a host of backward policies. What is the more likely choice, at home with a crying baby and a broken vacuum and a big easy-to-click Amazon button? The systems through which we obtain our stuff are vast and entrenched. This problem was bigger than my broken vacuum and the lack of a neighborhood fix-it shop. But stubborn and sleep-deprived, I wouldn't let go.

At home, I was drowning in clutter and broken stuff. But at work, which happened to be in the theatre, we fixed things all the time. I had worked for years as a set designer, and my husband, Michael, is a skilled technician and artisan. Backstage, if we need a specific lamp or dress or vacuum onstage and what we have doesn't work, we fix it. We are used to repairing, making, mending, improvising, and creatively problem-solving, on a tight budget. Could we put these two apparently unrelated worlds—the stuff at home and the stuff of the theatre—together?

I started big. I proposed to Michael that we write to Walmart and convince them to open a repair shop in the corner of every one of their stores, and that we, as theatre artists and vacuum owners, could help them figure this out. Michael was open to the idea, bless him, but reminded me that Walmart might not exactly be waiting for my call, and that perhaps it would be prudent to collect some data, some evidence that my ideas were appealing to other people, not just sleep-addled set designers with broken vacuums.

I saw the wisdom in that approach and turned my attention (temporarily!) to a smaller scale: I wondered if there was any way I could use our backstage theatre skills to both fix stuff and open a conversation in my local community about repair. But throughout, I was always thinking bigger, imagining what might happen if large manufacturers and retailers began (re)incorporating repair into their business models. What if there *were* a repair shop in the corner of every Walmart, Target, Home Depot, and IKEA? What if you could buy not only new goods in those places but also used goods? What if new stuff were designed in the first place so that it could be fixed? What would a better system look like—one that values stewardship over waste?

In June of 2013, baby Eric and preschooler Luke in tow, I launched Fixup, a locally grown experiment in creating alternatives to "use and discard." That June, and periodically for the next six years, Michael and I and a small group of theatre colleagues banded together to operate short-term pop-up repair shops in our neighborhood and other communities.

The premise was simple: Much like medieval itinerant tinkerers (and medieval theatre troupes), we would appear in a neighborhood storefront or farmers market for a limited amount of time, provide our services, and then move on. We would take the skills we commonly used in our backstage jobs—everything from carpentry and stitching to electrical work and soldering—and use them to fix people's everyday household items.

The longer-term goals were more ambitious. I wanted to know whether the practices and skills we habitually used in theatre had value in the real world. Was there a place in the modern world for the work of caring for our belongings? I wanted to find out whether people would have any interest in getting their stuff fixed. Was I alone in my rebellion against the broken toaster, the crammed apartment, and the multiplicity of frictionless paths toward the next online, fossil-fuel-delivered, cheap, shiny purchase? I wanted to talk with other people and find out if they were as unhappy with state of things as I was.

Personally, I wanted to *do* something. It felt hypocritical to bemoan our age of consumption and see my children overloaded at Christmas with present after plastic present from well-meaning and loving relatives—and even from me and my husband. As I scooped up bucketfuls of Legos from the floor, I began to feel, keenly and personally (and despite my efforts to shop responsibly, buy used, recycle, vote early and often, and so on), the inconsistency of our daily lives with our worries about the grim environmental realities I know my children will face when they grow up. The feeling of inaction was horrible: like watching a train coming down the tracks very slowly while we all sat on a blanket on the ties, enjoying a delicious tea party. By opening these repair shops and beginning to do something about a small piece of the problem, I wanted to try to take a step that might mean something to my kids and the rest of their generation in thirty years. It was one small first step—first steps are often small—and it wasn't going to solve everything overnight, but it felt good to attempt something concrete. I wanted to, just maybe, help tilt the world in the direction I hoped it would go.

And I wanted to sleep at night.

Pop Up Repair

This book flows from those first sleepless nights, that first pop-up repair shop, and the dozens of shops and events that followed. It shares insights culled from a few of the many objects, and their people, that we encountered during seven years of fixing, reusing, schlepping, and thinking about stuff. And it proposes a way forward: how we can have stuff, simply, without breaking the planet.

We operated that first pop-up in an empty storefront in Inwood, a neighborhood at the top of Upper Manhattan, a couple of blocks from our apartment. A local pharmacist rented it to us cheap, and we contacted a few friends and colleagues to see if they would join us and play repair shop for a month. I got a research grant from Barnard College, where I teach, to record data and document the event, and we crowdsourced $10,000 online to pay our fixers and our rent. I made a website, a logo, and got the necessary licenses from the city and state. We did grassroots outreach in the neighborhood, letting people know that we would fix all kinds of broken stuff. We had no idea what to charge, or whether people would be willing to pay. In June of 2013, I parked the now seven-month-old baby in an old ExerSaucer in the corner of our store, and we opened our doors for four weeks, unsure whether anyone would show up and, if they did, whether we'd actually be able to fix anything.

Well—they did, and we were.

People brought us all kinds of things to fix: lamps, chairs, blenders, toys, necklaces, ceramics. They brought things we'd never even heard of, like a polyester therapy tunnel, and things you might think never needed to exist, like a three-foot-tall gold plastic decorative ladle. And when they dropped off their Luxo lamps or pink scooters or stuffed lobsters to be fixed, they always told us about the item: where it came from, how they used it, why it broke, why they needed it. We called this "stuff therapy," and these interactions with customers, neighbors, friends, and family form the jumping-off point for each chapter of this book.

For I found, while listening to our customers talk about their stuff and struggling to fix it all, that there was a lot to be learned, not just about the lamps and the lobsters, or even the people who dropped them off, but about the way we humans make and use things, too, and how those things, in turn, help make us who we are.

The Story Continues

What is stuff? In 2007, Annie Leonard, an activist and now the executive director of Greenpeace USA, defined "stuff" as all the things in our homes that are not food: "iPods, clothes, shoes, cars, toasters, marshmallow shooters . . . Stuff we buy, maintain, lose, break, replace, stress about, and with which we confuse our personal self-worth." Leonard's social and environmental wake-up call, titled *The Story of Stuff*, helped to kick-start a growing awareness of the toll our Western habits of consumption take on the environment, on the communities where our stuff is made, and on our health. In case you need the stats, here are just a few of the inconvenient truths about how, as Leonard says, our consumption is "trashing the planet":

Household consumption represents up to 60 percent of global greenhouse gas (GHG) emissions and accounts for between 50 and 80 percent of total land, material, and water use. This includes our houses, our cars, our food, and our stuff. Of that household total, stuff represents 17 percent of emissions, and is the second-largest contributor to the "material footprint," that is to say, resource and raw materials extraction.[1] Put another way, by the US Environmental Protection Agency, "The extraction of natural resources; the production, transport, and disposal of goods, and the provision of services account for an estimated 29% of 2006 U.S. anthropogenic GHG emissions."[2]

Perhaps, like me, you are a bit numbed by the steady flow of grim climate change data, but the numbers are actually a story about real people and places. Our stuff overflows our landfills, litters our beaches, and degrades into an enormous Pacific garbage plastic soup bigger than Texas. Manufacturing our stuff has been implicated in health problems in communities around the world, shoddy labor practices, and such tragedies as the Rana Plaza collapse—the deadliest garment-factory accident in history. And if you live in the United States, it gets even uglier. More than a decade ago, Leonard warned that "the U.S. has 5% of the world's population but consumes 30% of the world's resources and creates 30% of the world's waste. If everybody consumed at U.S. rates, we would need 3 to 5 planets." And it hasn't gotten much better since then.[3]

In the past ten years, consumption by individuals in the United States has continued to grow steadily.[4] Even more important, emerging economies around the world are joining the fun. A World Resources Institute report titled "The Elephant in the Boardroom" projects that over the next fifteen years, more than three billion people will join the global middle class; that is, they will increasingly adopt American patterns of consumption. This has (to put it mildly) "long-term implications for environmental sustainability and, therefore, human and economic sustainability."[5]

When talking about environmental, human, and economic sustainability, we hear a lot, rightfully, about clean energy. Our system of consumption, like all our current economic systems, is powered by fossil fuels, and this needs to change. But clean energy is not enough. A report from the Ellen MacArthur Foundation states that transitioning to renewable energy and energy efficiency, while crucial, is not enough: "These measures can only address 55% of emissions. The remaining 45% comes from producing the cars, clothes, food, and other products we use every day. These cannot be overlooked."[6] The uncomfortable reality is that even if we somehow transition to renewable energy tomorrow, with a magical switch, we cannot pursue our current system of manufacture and consumption of goods without continuing to pay an unfathomable price in habitat destruction, resource depletion, and health hazards to manufacturing communities.

In addition to this dysfunction on a global scale, our patterns of consumption—that is, our relationships with our stuff—do not even make us happy on an individual level. People are increasingly frustrated by the system, and the way it manifests in their homes. I realized this early on during our first repair shop. I thought that our customers liked our shops because they wanted to reduce waste, to save the planet. But I quickly learned that their motivations for coming were much more personal, and sometimes very fraught. Many customers described a sense of being overwhelmed by clutter, or manipulated into buying something they didn't want. They disliked tossing perfectly good things, and expressed relief at finding our service. Beyond our shops, our society is fascinated with extremes—nightmares like the *Hoarders* television program or aspirational fantasies found in the pages of home magazines. And we struggle to find a healthy balance in our own homes.

You might credibly wonder, in the face of raging wildfires, hurricanes, madmen destroying the Amazon rain forest, global pandemic, and mass extinction (and not one of those examples is hyperbolic), whether consideration of our personal possessions—our blenders or vacuums, for crying out loud—matter one whit. And of course, in many ways, they don't. Not only are we and our blenders infinitesimal specks in a vast cosmic story that includes a heartbreaking (but only to us) blip called anthropocentric climate change, but there are many serious thinkers who have argued that what are sometimes dismissively called "personal lifestyle choices" don't matter, don't add up, and won't solve the climate crisis.

This line of thinking is counterproductive. It's true that individual, disconnected choices such as fixing a blender or buying organic lettuce will not, on their own, solve anything in the grand scheme of things. But negating the small actions we all take every day is dangerous because it implies that we can continue to live the way many of us currently do, or that we can make large systemic changes but somehow not have to change our own lives. Dismissals of "green" lifestyle choices, sometimes called conscious consumption, are predicated on the idea that individual action—especially about consumption—is somehow divorced from political action, or collective action. But each of us, with our dinky blenders and our differing carbon footprints and our mundane daily decisions, contributes to those vast, staggering, overwhelmingly collective numbers. Together, our individual actions add up to collective actions—to our culture. And the choices we make in our daily lives influence the choices we make as families, as communities, and ultimately, influence the choices we make at the ballot box, where we can come together to scale and multiply those many individual choices.

It is true that we won't fix climate change if we simply rely on individuals to choose to buy organic soap or "green" products. We need political and systemic changes, we need different incentive structures for businesses and municipalities, we need to address the grotesque inequality that make it difficult for many to have real individual choices, and we need to rethink economic and cultural assumptions surrounding value, labor, and growth. But we can not make false distinctions between systems and the individuals who inhabit and define them, because they are, in fact, deeply intertwined. And because by and large, thirteen years after *The Story of Stuff*, we are still living in a linear system defined by massive manufacture, rapid consumption, and heedless disposal of consumer goods. But there are signs of change—for individuals, and for the larger systems we live within.

The Stuff Movement

A few weeks after our first pop-up, which as you will recall was a scrappy one-month stint at a former pharmacy in our not-particularly-fashionable neighborhood, we were shocked to receive an invitation to appear on an MSNBC cable news program. Apparently, we had hit a nerve. We screwed up our courage and went on the show to talk about what I called a burgeoning "stuff movement." In the years since that first pop-up, the national conversation about stuff has begun a marked shift. The stuff movement was in its infancy when we opened that first shop, and is still very young. But it is happening, and people are hungry for it.

Just look at the wildfire response to Marie Kondo's *The Life-Changing Magic of Tidying Up*. People couldn't get enough of a thoughtful, practical, and refreshing guide for how to deal with all their crap. Kondo's clear, heartfelt, and gently delivered but spanking-firm advice resonated with millions, as do various other stuff prescriptions, including minimalism, home organizing, zero-waste lifestyles, and simplicity guides.

But the problem with Marie Kondo, and minimalism, and many other proposed solutions (perhaps even the quick fix of a short-term repair shop), is that for the most part they represent a kind of extreme makeover—the juice cleanses of the home goods world. They might work to get us on the right track, but purging and organizing your home are massive (and hopefully rare) undertakings. This type of radical, one-size-fits-all solution—like radical, one-size-fits-all diets—may serve as an emergency intervention or a reset, but is not a strategy for the long haul.

Stuff Is Just Like Food

I make the analogy to diet crazes for a reason. In building a more comprehensive and long-term stuff movement, we can learn a lot from our food.

Forty or fifty years ago, significant numbers of people in this country began connecting the dots between our mechanized, linear, industrial food system and negative personal, social, and environmental health impacts, and those people began exploring avenues for change. Those thinkers and activists and farmers and artists and dropouts and cooks and just plain people who liked food began the food movement—an inchoate and multiheaded beast that's still got a long way to go but has, at the very least, raised an awareness that what we put into our bodies affects our health, our happiness, the health of the people who grow and harvest our food, and last but certainly not least, the health of our shared planet.

Well, stuff is a lot like food. The objects we make and bring into our homes are harvested and produced from the bounty of the earth and shaped by human hands, human labor—even if that labor is increasingly automated. We bring these objects into our homes, and they shape our daily lives, the rhythm of our days. Your lamp lights your family dinner, your coffee maker marks your morning routine. The things around us create a story of who we are, and they impact our health and happiness and planet just as our food does.

Michael Pollan, food writer—food guru—developed a simple axiom regarding how to eat: "Eat food. Not too much. Mostly plants."[7] I propose that we adapt this wisdom for our belongings: Have good stuff (not too much), mostly reclaimed. Care for it. Pass it on.

Yes, my version is a little bit longer. I'll explain why. It has to do with our very last pop-up.

Pop Up Journey

In 2018, after fixing thousands of broken objects, I wanted to try something a little different. During the first five years of the pop-ups, I had juggled the project along with my "regular" work as a theatrical set designer and a professor at Barnard College. I would design a show, then run a repair shop, then another show, all the while teaching my classes in the Theatre Department and taking on the work of building a climate action program at Barnard (plus raising two kids). It sounds cuckoo, and at times it felt that way too. Thankfully, all this juggling was in partnership with the ever-steadfast Michael and, rather amazingly, with support and encouragement from my colleagues at Barnard, which is the kind of institution that is willing to embrace the unconventional and help its people grow. At parties, when people asked me what I did, I had to either pick one (designer, teacher, repair entrepreneur, climate activist) or buttonhole the poor person who was just trying to be polite while I explained how these disparate professional threads were in fact all related. Because to me, they certainly were.

By early 2019, we had operated more than a dozen short-term shops across New York City, hosted scores of educational events, fixed thousands of items, been covered in the press by organizations from the *New York Times* to local papers to Japanese TV. We had gotten up at the crack of dawn countless times to rent a van and move broken (or fixed) items around the city. I had shivered in our repair tents at wintry farmers markets, darning sweaters and listening to customers share their stories, their frustrations, and their hopes. I had begun speaking and writing about our experiences, I had changed the way I designed, and I taught a class at Barnard called Things and Stuff. "Baby Eric" was now a six-year-old.

My own feelings of frustration with stuff had given way to something more complex, more thoughtful, and ultimately easier. While the problems of stuff still existed, they felt less overwhelming and more clearly interconnected. I decided to create an event that would connect the dots between repair and the rest of the cycle of consumption.

We found a storefront again, this time in the Seaport District all the way downtown, and made a sign for the front that said GOOD STUFF. Compared with our earlier pop-ups, it was a much fancier spot with higher rent, but we were still just a scrappy team trying to make something real out of an idea—a bunch of theatre kids, playing. We created a "home" in our storefront, with a living room, dining room, bedroom, closets, and a repair shop in the back. I painted my adapted version of Michael Pollan's food axiom on the walls: HAVE GOOD STUFF (NOT TOO MUCH), MOSTLY RECLAIMED. CARE FOR IT. PASS IT ON. And we opened for business—a one-month exploration of how we can do stuff better, from new to used to fixed all the way to the end of life of an object.

This book is organized around those central principles of how to have good stuff. Using a few of the thousands of objects we encountered in our pop-up journey to illustrate each step, its chapters propose a path forward that recognizes the role of the individual, the community, businesses, good policy, and just a little faith in our capacity to repair a broken system.

Have Good Stuff (Not Too Much), Mostly Reclaimed. Care for It. Pass It On.

This axiom (and the practices it invites) is familiar and, lovingly, somewhat recycled. Much of what we did in our repair shops was "innovative" only in that it recombined time-tested practices in unusual ways. It certainly wasn't glamorous, and it wasn't necessarily high tech. Like Michael Pollan's food guidelines, a healthy relationship with stuff is simple, it's common sense, it's what we probably learned from our grandmothers. But that's exactly why it's in danger of getting lost in the noise, in the constant push for new shiny toys and silver bullet solutions. Calling for a return to repair, maintenance, and quality might seem hopelessly old-fashioned. Can't we just throw all our broken, used-up stuff into a big machine somewhere and extract the materials? Isn't there some high-tech fix? Maybe. Or maybe we need to reclaim a certain kind of neglected wisdom, and adapt it for the moment we are living in today.[8]

And that's really why you are reading these words. It's not only because my toaster broke. It's not only because I am a designer and teacher and repair-shop entrepreneur who has made and fixed and schlepped thousands of objects over the years. It's also because I am convinced that making and having stuff are as central to our species as language, as cooked food, as collaboration, as dress, as art. And that no matter how much we minimize or simplify, we humans will always have and use stuff. So we've got to find a way to do it better.

The good news is, we have the tools. We can build a better, circular model of care, of stewardship, of maintenance. A model where we value what we have.

Stuff is broken.

Let's fix it.

PART I

HAVE GOOD STUFF

Why do we have (and keep) stuff? And what makes (some) stuff good?

You might go for minimalist sleek shelves with books sorted by the color of the spine, or you might like a bit of clutter and keep a comprehensive collection of lace Kleenex box cozies. You might live in an apartment or an RV or a tree house or even a sleeping bag—whatever floats your boat. But there's no escaping the fact that human beings have stuff. It's fundamental to our species; it's part of who we are. As we contemplate our overstuffed sock drawers and the plastic vortex in our oceans, it is important to accept that having stuff is something we need to do as human beings—and face the reality that it's something we need to do better. In order to achieve that, we need to better understand our options and learn how to find the good stuff.

It's easier to define good stuff in the negative, by exploring some of the items we repaired that were eminently not good. Perhaps unfairly, it is uncooperative items like these that stood out in our shop, like unruly children in a schoolroom squawking and demanding all our time while the easily fixed, well-behaved items slip out of mind more easily. Nothing distressed us more than these "repair fails," the vast majority of which fell into the small appliance category, largely for reasons of design, material choice, and availability of parts. As we discovered, unfixable items have many things in common, and as a whole, the things that make a product "good" also tend to mean that it will be repairable. Good stuff is well designed for a long life cycle, made of the right materials, has parts that are easily available and replaceable, and was produced in a socially and environmentally ethical process. Good stuff may, at times, cost more—but not always.

CHAPTER 1:

Our (Long and Tangled) Story of Stuff

But lo! Men have become the tools of their tools.
—Henry David Thoreau

Karen H. was one of our first customers. She showed up with a backpack that had a small tear, which we stitched shut at our table at the local farmers market. She later returned to our storefront in a nearby former pharmacy with a set of window blinds and two identical shower radios. The shower radios were among the first of many projects brought to our shops that puzzled us. Why did Karen have at home not one but two identical broken shower radios? Why did she hold on to them—perhaps on the off chance some kooky theatre people might one day open an experimental repair shop in her neighborhood? Why not just buy a new one? You can order a shower radio on Amazon for $12.97.

Karen's shower radios illustrate her—and our—seemingly irrational attachment to the things we own. And I'm not talking about antiques or family heirlooms or your childhood blanky. Those things make sense, somewhat, in their rarity or connection to emotionally charged events. The shower radios will help tell us why we are also attached to some of the most boring and anonymous things in our lives and, indeed, why we have stuff in the first place.

It might seem easy to dismiss Karen as a probable crackpot or weird hoarder, and to imagine her at home fiddling with the dials of her broken shower radios, outdated issues of the *New Yorker* stacked knee high, perhaps barking her shin on a gramophone as she fights her way to the front door. But I'm pretty sure Karen is not a hoarder; we all hold on to things, as we saw time and time again in our shops. People brought all kinds of things that seemed eminently replaceable, mundane, meaningless. They arrived with black plastic fans, homely toasters, single wooden chairs with wobbly joints, cheap costume pearls with the finish flaking off, a little plastic toy bee with a broken leg (all the way from Staten Island). It's not possible that all these people were hoarders, incapable of "rational" behavior regarding their stuff.

At first, green crusaders that we were, we thought that people came to our little shop to save the planet. In Karen's case, we fixed one of the two shower radios. One radio had a broken antenna we could not reattach, but the second had corroded battery contacts that we were able to clean, and the radio hummed back to life. So, assuming Karen wanted or needed two shower radios in her life and would have bought new ones without our intervention, we prevented the extraction of resources required to make one shower radio, the carbon emissions to ship it, and the landfill space for the final remains of the old one. We imagined that this green savings was what brought Karen to our shop in the first place. But it turns out that Karen, honest soul, did not use our service to save the planet. Nor did most everyone else. We conducted a survey during our first pop-up, and asked customers a series of questions about their motivations, including

- On a scale of 1–10, did you come in today / use repair for yourself or the planet (1 = planet, 10 = yourself)?

- On a scale of 1–10, was your motivation for using repair to reduce waste or to have a working object again? (1 = reduce waste, 10 = working object)?
- On a scale of 1–10, rate yourself as an environmentalist (1 = not at all, 10 = strong environmentalist).

Karen's answers were as follows: *10*, she came for herself, not the planet; *10*, she came to have the object working again, not to reduce waste; and *1*, she was not at all an environmentalist. She just wanted, if possible, to have *her* shower radios work again, and not to have to get new ones. Even more interesting, the people who rated themselves as strong environmentalists still reported that their motivation was not waste reduction: they just wanted their object to work again.

But it wasn't quite that simple. In addition to wanting their stuff to work, people often seemed to feel a need to talk about their object when they brought it in: stuff therapy. They told us, of course, what wasn't working. This is the bare minimum exchange between a fixer and a customer: we have to know what is wrong, what the object should do or be that it isn't doing or being. But people often shared far more than the bare minimum. We learned where they got it, and why, where it lived in their home, how long it had been broken, how it broke, and why it mattered to them. Sometimes they told us explicitly why they cared about it; sometimes we could read between the lines. Karen, for example, was straightforward: she liked to listen to the radio in the shower, and she liked the way that particular radio worked. She had her routines and she was sticking to them.

Sometimes the motivation was more complex. Steve C., for example, always had a great (and revealing) tale to tell when dropping off his numerous items. In the case of his Chinese scroll wall hanging, he had been play-fighting with his son and somehow the wall hanging had gotten caught in the middle; the paper was torn off the dowel. His wife was irritated, apparently, and Steve's somewhat sheepish delivery of the wall hanging to our shop seemed to be a mild form of penance. Steve lit up when we handed him his fixed scroll and marched off with a relieved and hopeful air as if, perhaps, he might be working on a problem bigger than a broken wall hanging.

Many customers, of course, wanted to save money: usually fixing the item is cheaper than buying a new one. Sometimes we couldn't beat the price of a new item—for example, certain small appliances like hair dryers and electric toothbrushes, which tend to be inexpensive to purchase but time consuming to fix. In these cases, some people did balk at our prices. But money was clearly not the only motivation for many customers, especially in the relatively comfortable New York neighborhoods where we operated several of our shops—and often even in the less affluent areas. There were many times when our repair prices were surprisingly close to or even above a replacement cost, but people still chose to repair. People felt that their items were not, technically, replaceable—even when similar items were available online for $12.97, while the repair cost $20. The motivation to keep our stuff is not only environmental, or financial. It is emotional—maybe even irrational.

The rationality assumption in economics is based on the idea that people will choose options that most benefit their self-interest. However, as many studies have shown, and we all have observed with our own two eyes, rationality is not actually the best means of predicting human behavior.[1] For example, compulsive hoarding in its medical definition is inherently an irrational behavior, but it is nonetheless on the rise. Hoarding was given that medical diagnosis relatively recently, in 2013, the same year we launched our first pop-up. And while keeping and repairing two arguably unnecessary shower radios isn't hoarding, Karen might have been fairly accused of irrationality, at least on the face of it. But when we look more closely, she may have had some very deep-seated and sensible reasons for keeping her stuff. Indeed, perhaps it is a society that makes it impossible for people to keep their stuff in good working order that should be labeled irrational. As Kurt Vonnegut is reported to have said, "A sane person to an insane society must appear insane." After all, Karen, with her irrational attachment to stuff, is in very good company: most of the human race.

The Caillou and the Clever Cro-Magnon

One perspective on the roots of our irrational behavior regarding stuff popped up in an unlikely place, as things often do during a bit of time off, far away from shower radios or pop-ups or work of any kind. The summer following our tenth repair shop, Michael and I took our sons to France. My mother is French, and Michael's father lives there, so we try to spend time there during the summer as often as we can. It's always hot, almost always sunny, and a treasured time to reconnect to our childhood summers. We often take side trips, departing from the well-worn paths of family meals and kids' summer routines to see a bit of the country, from Roman amphitheatres to the beaches of Normandy.

That year, I found myself on a bench in a fierce dry heat, the cicadas singing their deafening chorus. A young French historian addressed herself mainly to a row of children, who were seated cross-legged on leather hides in front of benches packed with parents and a few overheated toddlers. We were at a famous French prehistoric cave site, participating to various degrees in a workshop on how to knap flint. While the parents fanned themselves and the toddlers squirmed, the dozen or so children were fully engaged, hoping they might leave with some spears or at least a nice chunk of flint with which to poke one another.

The docent opened with a simple question, in French: "What is the first and simplest tool used by *l'homme préhistorique*?" The English- and German-speaking kids fidgeted uncomprehendingly; they had signed up to watch someone banging rocks together and were already losing patience. One little French boy raised his hand and declared that a spear was the earliest tool. The historian gently, but with just a touch of disapprobation, reminded him that a spear requires a lot of work to make. The answer she was looking for was much simpler, and was offered by a thoughtful twelve-year-old girl wearing glasses and a purple sun visor: "*une pierre, un caillou.*" A rock, a simple stone.

A ripple ran through the kids. . . . *Yes, finally, now we are getting to it. Shall we start banging them together?* They sat up a bit straighter. But, no, more talking. . . . Encouraged by the docent, the group collectively noted that a lot of other animals use this type of simple tool—birds, bugs, monkeys. (My son Luke offered up the sea otter as a prime example of a stone-tool-using animal prodigy, knowledge gained after hours of diligent observation of *Wild Kratts* nature shows.) The young French historian pointed out, however, that the real difference between the early human and these other animals is not necessarily the *use* of the simple *caillou*, but that, having cracked his almond or accessed his bone marrow, the early human might keep his rock and save it for the next meal, while the monkey or otter would drop his tool and find a new one next time. So, using the rock in the first place, that's one thing, but to put the rock in your pocket just in case: "*Alors ça, c'est malin!*" Now, that's clever! According to her, it is this particular cleverness—keeping stuff—that is distinctively human.

Holding on to the rock she found today, your average Cro-Magnon might encounter another almond or bone to be split tomorrow—and she'd be prepared. Perhaps, then, it makes perfect sense that a twenty-first-century human might also feel the urge to hold on to stuff just in case. Why not keep those too-small ice skates at the back of the closet? They'd certainly be useful if that ice rink ever reopens. (Maybe with thin socks?) And that djembe drum—boy, that could really come in handy someday. . . .

This connection to things beyond the present moment or immediate needs is part of what anthropologist Ian Hodder has called "human-thing entanglement." Hodder argues that not only is dependence on things "inherent to the human species," but that the things we make and use draw us into a web of dependence and care, which leads to more things and draws us into more dependence on them, ad infinitum in an ever-expanding web:

> Human "being" is thoroughly dependent on made things. Since the first tool, humans have always dealt with problems by changing things. This dependence on things has produced our "humanity," but it has also entrapped us in yet greater dependence. Things are unstable: They have their own processes that entangle humans into their care.[2]

In the beginning, however, our entanglement was limited in scale by our technology and our need to stay mobile: "You could place on a small table all the material belongings of a man or woman who lived thirty thousand years ago. They had very little stuff."[3] This does not mean that we should assume that our Cro-Magnon friend is more virtuous than we are, with our useless skates and aspirational djembe drums. As anthropologist Daniel Miller argues, it's a fallacy to romanticize earlier or so-called simpler societies as somehow better (or worse) in terms of stuff:

> [The] model of the noble, unmaterialistic savage is entirely unhelpful. All it achieves is an assumption of lost purity. It makes

us feel alienated and polluted simply for being who we are . . . we too are stuff, and our use and identification with material culture provides a capacity for enhancing, just as much as for submerging, our humanity.[4]

However, while all humans, everywhere, may be entangled with our things, we are not at all equal in terms of sheer volume. With today's American homes and garages and storage units, our distinctive human ability to make and keep things, baked into our DNA over hundreds of thousands of years, becomes excessive, at times grotesque. Having learned the evolutionary advantage to keeping our stuff (as a means to get a leg up on sea otters and apes and precocious birds on YouTube), we amplify this basic human tendency with the power of modern technology to make more stuff, send it all over the world, and build storage units for it.

All human societies, whether traveling light or yoked to massive McMansions crammed with recent Amazon acquisitions, depend on things, just as we depend on food. The paradox, therefore, is to accept this fundamental dimension of our humanity, while acknowledging the environmental destruction and social inequality that our tangled web of stuff connects us to—and somehow, fix it. Hodder explicitly warns about the human tendency to try to "fix" things with yet more technology and more things, which only expands the entanglement: "We cannot keep doing what we have always done—find short-term technological solutions that lock us into long-term pathways." Instead, he recommends that we try to begin to see the "thingness of things," that is to say, to see our relationship with things in a new light. Now, if it is not instantly crystal clear to you how exactly to embrace the thingness of things, we already have a useful example from, you guessed it, the world of food.

Subjects, Objects, and the Flow of Things

We tend to think of ourselves, either as individuals or as a species, as the central character in what we accordingly call "the human drama." We are the subjects of the story, and animals, plants, and most certainly *things* do not have a big role, or really a role at all other than perhaps as props. In *The Botany of Desire*, Michael Pollan turned our view of the relationship between plants and humans upside down, recasting plants, usually seen as mute and passive, as crafty colonizers who exploit human tastes and labor to proliferate all over the globe. Rather than the object of our desires or tastes ("we grow corn, we eat corn, we like corn") the plant is understood as the subject of its own narrative. Corn uses *us* for its own evolutionary success.

Similarly, we might broaden our sense of who is subject and who is object in the person-thing lexicon. Generally—it's embedded in the very language—things are seen as objects, and we are the subjects: I hammer the nail, I drive the car, I break the shower radio. Hodder's entanglement theory opens the possibility that, at the very least, it is more of a two-way street than we might think. We drive the car, but the car also demands a relationship of care, of washing, of filling with gas, of digging old Cheerios out from between the seats. Even further, the car draws us into a web of relationships with other things and people—the parts and labor required to make it, the potential uses for the materials reclaimed when the car is salvaged, the things that we transport in the trunk. There are times we might even feel that, as with plants, the presumed subject-object relationship between humans and things can become reversed. As anyone who has spent a day trying to empty out a storage unit or clean up a kid's room will know, we now live in a world where many people have so much stuff that it can seem impossible to deal with it all. It can sometimes feel like our stuff owns *us*, demanding so much care and maintenance in our entangled relationship that it is not always clear who, or what, is in charge.

The possibility surfaced by Pollan, Hodder, and in our repair shops, is not to struggle for control over our stuff, but to recognize our relationship with things as interdependent and more complex than we might think. And a repair shop, as it turns out, may be a uniquely appropriate environment for examining the complexities of the human-thing relationship. Bill Brown, who like Hodder is an anthropologist-theorist, contends that we normally do not really perceive the things around us—until they stop working. It is only when they are unable to perform their function, when they fail to be obedient objects to our subjects, that we really see them as themselves:

> We begin to confront the thingness of objects when they stop working for us: when the drill breaks, when the car stalls, when the windows get filthy, when their flow within the circuits of production and distribution, consumption and exhibition, has been arrested, however momentarily.[5]

In Brown's example, when the window is clean (fixed), we see *through* it. When it is dirty (broken), we actually see the window itself as a *thing*, instead of an object. When the window stops performing its function in relation to our needs, only then do we begin to recognize it as a thing that exists outside of its service to us. And it is in the imperfect satisfaction of our desires that we are stopped, caught short and made aware of our own dependence. When an object breaks, we begin to see that we live in a relationship with our things. They fulfill our needs, but they have needs as well. And when that relationship breaks down, because of dirt, or accident, or corroded battery contacts, it impacts not only the flow of "production and distribution, consumption and exhibition," but also the flow of our lives.

This idea of flow, of the smoothness of our days as we might like them to unfold, reveals another component of our relationship with things. When we wake up and turn on the radio, look through the window, or brew the coffee, those actions, however small, are part of what defines and shapes the rhythm of our daily lives. When the shower radio or coffee machine fails, the flow of our morning is interrupted, however momentarily, creating a sense of frustration, a lack of control, a perception of the precariousness of our many human-thing entanglements. Our attention is drawn to the thing that interrupted the flow, and we look for a solution, a resumption of the smooth life we intend to lead, rather than the precarious reality we live in.

This interruption to the flow of our daily life may threaten something even deeper: our sense of who we are. Miller argues that our stuff is not simply the result, or even a reflection of, some "true" inner self, but that we actually create our identities with our material choices. In this passage, he refers to clothing, but his idea applies to all the objects we surround ourselves with, in body and home:

> It is as though if we peeled off the outer layers, we would finally get to the real self within. . . . Actually, as Ibsen's Peer Gynt observed, we are all onions. If you keep peeling off our layers you find— absolutely nothing left. There is no true inner self. . . . The clothes were not superficial, they actually were what made us what we think we are.[6]

So, when an item breaks and interrupts the flow of our day, it also interrupts our sense of who we are. All of a sudden, our irrational attachments start to seem, if not more rational, at least more understandable as deeply connected to our sense of self.

Faced with this interruption to our carefully constructed identities, one obvious solution, for many, is a new shower radio. But we have clearly seen in our shops that there are often times, even for people living at the height of the consumer society, when that solution doesn't feel right. Our customers found us because *a specific, particular* object worked for them—and they wanted it to continue working. They have a relationship with that thing, that backpack or radio—even that little *caillou* or rock—because it fits into the flow of their life; it is part of their daily routine, and part of their perception of who they are in the world. And a new one doesn't quite feel the same.

Basic Human Stuff

It may seem like a stretch to attribute Karen's trip to our little repair shop to her sense of identity, or her basic membership in the human race. But owning and keeping tools and things is one of the few habits and traits that *all* human cultures have in common. We all have language, clothing, religion, art, cooked food—and stuff we make with other stuff (our tools). And unlike otters or birds, we keep our tools, and serve them so that they can serve us. Feeling connected, entangled, and intertwined with our stuff is part of who we are on both the individual and the species level. It makes sense that we place value and meaning on the things we own, even when they are cheap plastic radios. We have stuff because it is not only part of the flow of how we live and how we survive but also who we are.

But our increasingly encumbered society does not make it easy for people to maintain that flow, to keep their stuff working, and to take care of the things they value, however mundane or small they might be. We'll unpack *why* our society makes it so hard to care for what we have in other chapters. But the starting point is realizing that the drive to have and keep stuff, be it shower radios or stone axes, runs deep in the DNA of our species, in every aspect of our daily lives, and in our understanding of who we are in the world. Once we begin to understand the things in our lives a bit more fully, to rethink the relationship between subject and object, then we can begin to think about the whole system differently, and can imagine a system that might work better for all—for Karen, for all of us, and for the planet.

CHAPTER 2:

The Good, the Bad, and the Ugly Truth about How Stuff Got That Way

> *The work of the world is common as mud*
> *Botched, it smears the hands, crumbles to dust.*
> *But the thing worth doing well done*
> *has a shape that satisfies, clean and evident.*
> *Greek amphoras for wine or oil,*
> *Hopi vases that held corn, are put in museums*
> *but you know they were made to be used.*
> *The pitcher cries for water to carry*
> *and a person for work that is real.*
> —Marge Piercy, from "To be of use"

In our very first pop-up, we were naïve enough to accept cell phones, digital cameras, tablets, and other digital products for repair. None of us was especially into fixing these items, but since the ethos of the shop was "come one, come all, and bring whatever you've got that's broken," it seemed appropriate to try to tackle the world of screens. My husband,

Michael—who for better or worse had the patience and skill to figure out almost anything—spent some time on YouTube and learned how to change phone screens, replace batteries, and use an iFixit "liberation kit," a cute little screwdriver set that matches the very uncute little proprietary screws that Apple uses to keep people from opening their phones. That should have tipped us off right there. For a fixer, ease of access to the innards of an item is paramount: if you must spend extra time and have a special tool just to get inside the thing, chances are it was not designed with easy, accessible repair in mind.

But we were young(ish) and foolish, and so we accepted these items for those first few weeks. One day, Michael pushed away from his workbench with a rare show of anger and declared an end to digital repair in our shop: he was over it. I walked over to see what had sent him off the edge and found him with an iPad that belonged to our friend and neighbor, Andy. Andy, innocently and dutifully supporting our little shop, and perhaps because his tweenage daughter, Izzy, liked to work behind the front desk, had brought us his iPad with a broken screen.

Michael had discovered, the hard way, that Andy's iPad was almost impossible to repair. iFixit, an online repair kit vendor and leader in tech repair activism, gave the 2013 iPad a score of 2/10 for repairability.[1] The most recent version has the same low score; everything is glued down so there is a high chance of cracking the screen during disassembly, and the glue makes removing a broken screen like Andy's a sharp, nasty mess.[2] After long hours hunched over the workbench scraping off shards of glued-on broken screen, Michael finally got the new screen installed, only to find that the whole thing worked except for one letter—the letter *K*, as it turned out. Unable to imagine telling a customer (even a friend) that he could use his iPad but that, unfortunately, he could not type the letter *K*, Michael began all over again. This type of occasional redo is one of the bummers of repair, but would have been mitigated if the process of changing out the screen were not so infernal. Once you get inside that beautiful iPad, it is clear that it was carefully designed either with complete disregard for making it possible to change the screen easily or, worse, to purposefully make it difficult to do so.

The Whole Apple

Apple is of course famous for designing beautiful things. Over the past four decades, the company liberated personal computing from the early boxy deskbound objects that resembled HVAC units and released a cascade of sleek, playful, almost sensual products that populate the waking (and increasingly, sleeping) lives of people all over the world— with more than 1.4 billion devices active as of 2019.[3] A commitment to careful, even obsessive, aesthetics drove this process, led both by the iconic Steve Jobs and the less well known but equally influential Jony Ive, Apple's chief design guru from 1996 to 2019. Apple products have been rightly heralded as having shaped much of the design aesthetic of the past two decades, and not only in the area of personal computing, smartphones, and digital products. Apple products are featured at the Museum of Modern Art, and have influenced the design of everything from minimalist white glasses frames to Yotel lobbies that look as if you should swipe on them to EVE, the cute but terrifyingly powerful futuristic robot in Pixar's 2008 film *WALL-E*.

WALL-E follows the title character, a dirty but adorable robot who resembles a toaster oven crossed with a toy tractor, valiantly working to clean up a grotesquely spoiled Earth covered with human trash. Ironically, WALL-E's love interest and partner in saving the earth is EVE, who from a design point of view is basically a white 2006 MacBook crossed with a penguin. This resemblance is not coincidental; Jony Ive consulted on the EVE prototype at the request of Steve Jobs. The irony lies in the fact that Apple's design practices have in fact yielded two results. The first, already noted, is the beauty, simplicity, and power of its products and its subsequent global ubiquity. The second result is an enormous, enormous amount of waste.

It's hard to calculate what percentage of the nearly fifty million tons of e-waste created globally each year can be traced back to Apple.[4] It's possible, however, to get a sense of the probable scale of the Apple waste that a real-world WALL-E might be up against. Of the 1.4 billion active Apple devices worldwide in 2019, nine hundred million were phones. Most iPhones weigh at least five ounces, with newer models weighing up to half a pound.[5] Assuming a conservative average weight of six ounces, that means there are 337 million pounds of potential Apple waste in phones alone in use right now around the globe, which is equivalent to about half the weight of the Empire State Building. This does not even account for all the phones and devices that have already been sent to landfills or taken apart for materials by people working in unsafe conditions around the world.

What about recycling and refurbishing and trade-in? Surely not all of that half an Empire State Building's worth of phones goes into the trash? You might argue that Apple takes back its phones, and even offers repair services at its Genius Bars. (The astute among you might have asked why on earth Andy didn't go to a Genius Bar to get his iPad fixed.) Well, here are some uncomfortable truths about those two options.

Apple advertises that

> through Apple Trade In, customers in 27 countries can trade in their devices either online or in-store. For products that still have more to give, customers can receive an Apple Store Gift Card or a refund on their purchase. These devices are repaired when necessary and sent to their next owner. If a product is at the end of its life, we'll recycle it for free. We also collect and refurbish used devices through our iPhone Upgrade Program, AppleCare, and, inside Apple, our Hardware Reuse Program for employees. Altogether, we directed 7,860,000 devices to new users in fiscal year 2018.

Those 7.8 million refurbished devices represent less than 2.8 percent of the total sold in 2018.[6]

It's almost impossible to get good figures on third-party refurbishment and resale, which would account for another small percentage, but globally, e-waste is recycled at a rather dismal 16 percent. Apple touts the fifty-three thousand tons of waste it diverted from its operations in 2018, but that figure is dwarfed by the weight of its actual product going into the waste stream.[7] Most important, the weight of the phone itself is a trifling percentage of the energy and resources used—and waste created—in manufacturing all those new phones (and, in fact, all our stuff). In a 2002 ecological design manifesto, *Cradle to Cradle*, William McDonagh and Michael Braungart point out that that "what most people see in their garbage cans is just the tip of a material iceberg: the product itself contains on average only 5 percent of the raw materials involved in making and delivering it."[8] Annie Leonard writes that for every pound tossed into landfill, at least seventy pounds of waste are created in manufacturing new goods.[9] Any way you slice it, making all those new phones means creating a lot of garbage—and a lot of GHG emissions.

Those emissions, like the physical waste, come mainly from making so much new stuff. In 2017, Apple reported 27.5 million metric tons of carbon emissions, which is equal to the emissions from 5.9 million cars on the road in one year. Seventy-seven percent of those emissions come from manufacturing. The company's sustainability report includes several glossy pages on switching to renewable energy in its corporate facilities, which is a good thing. Unfortunately, corporate facilities represent only 1 percent of the company's total footprint. The report does acknowledge that whopping 77 percent, and details plans to work with suppliers to switch *those* facilities to renewable energy. Also good news—but unfortunately, the carbon savings in 2017 from that work with suppliers totaled only 320,000 metric tons of CO_2, another 1 percent of the total.

To its credit, Apple is starting to talk about "closing the loop" in terms of materials—reclaiming some of those millions of pounds of trash in order to reduce more effectively those millions of tons of carbon. Perhaps inspired by WALL-E and EVE, Apple created two real-world robots to fight waste. Liam and his successor, Daisy, can disassemble iPhones and sort components, "so we can recover more materials at a higher quality than traditional recyclers can."[10] In addition to making recycling look cool with Daisy, Apple has accomplished the almost impossible task of making repair and service look sexy, at least at the front desk, in the form of its glossy temples, a.k.a. Genius Bars. Daisy and the Genius Bars look pretty cool, but don't be seduced just yet. The company does not provide any statistics on how many devices its geniuses repair annually. And as for the more artificial geniuses, for now, Daisy's capacity is still limited. And while Apple is using some reclaimed aluminum and other recycled materials, with a stated goal of "no new mined materials," it is not saying how much of its current products are made from reclaimed materials. Finally, all the Genius Bars or even robots in the world won't make it significantly easier to remove a glued-on screen. Apple has prioritized certain aspects of design, especially newness and aesthetic appeal, over others like longevity, accessibility, and modularity. The fact of the matter is that the fundamental design of the iPhone and the iPad still takes a linear approach, based on a business model built on selling more new stuff, more often.

In other words, Apple's waste and emissions are designed right into the products along with the smooth lines and sophisticated colors. A 2015 *New Yorker* profile of Ive, written by Ian Parker, quotes the Apple designer as saying that "so much of our manufactured environment testifies to carelessness." Ive is presumably referring to poor design, not e-waste. However, there is little evidence that Ive or his team acknowledge the link between design and waste. Parker presses the Apple team: "Today, Apple's designers, like their competitors, make machines that are almost disposable: the screens crack; the processors become outmoded.

I asked if this caused discomfort, and there was a pause. . . . Earlier, Ive had said that he wouldn't trade reach for permanence" because the Apple design studio's perpetual advancements improved "the quality of life for millions and millions and millions of people." There is no men-tion of the quality of life of the pickers who sort e-waste in Southeast Asia, of the miners who extract the tin, tungsten, and gold found in an iPhone, and of the millions—perhaps billions—of us who have perhaps unwittingly traded the health of our water, our fellow humans, and our planet for the admittedly wondrous power granted us by our phones.[11]

But is this trade-off even necessary? The implication is that it is impossible for a company to have "reach"—to have customers across the world using its products, to influence the look and feel of an era, and ultimately to grow its business—without creating enormous amounts of waste and human suffering. This pernicious idea has its roots in con-cepts formulated more than a century ago in business and advertising circles, called obsolescence.

All Roads Lead to Obsolescence

The term "planned obsolescence" is often associated with Bernard Lon-don, a real estate agent who in 1932 self-published a series of essays that called for ending the Depression through a centralized government program that would curtail the life span of consumer goods. In Lon-don's plan, at the end of a predetermined amount of time, manufac-tured objects would be "legally 'dead,'" and recalled. People would then buy new goods, "and the wheels of industry would be kept going and employment regularized and assured for the masses."[12]

While London envisioned government regulation as the mechanism for determining the end of life for a product, in the ensuing century it is largely corporations—and the designers who work for them—that have taken on the job of determining the life span of a product. And while London imagined that the government would explicitly "assign a lease of life to shoes and homes and machines," with "the term of their existence definitely known by the consumer," in today's version of London's vision, the term of existence is determined by more subtle factors: software that inexplicably slows down after certain updates,[13] batteries that can't be replaced,[14] and screens that are glued on. All these design decisions remove the need for London's centrally determined end of life, and, even better, remove the need to tell your customer about it. The end of life is baked into the product from the start, but well hidden. The result, however, is the same as London hoped: new products are "constantly pouring forth from the factories and marketplaces, to take the place of the obsolete" and the "wheels of industry" keep turning.

There is another, equally powerful tool for greasing the wheels of industry. Three years before London's now-famous article was published, Christine Frederick, a "home efficiency expert" and author, produced *Selling Mrs. Consumer*, a 434-page book dedicated to Herbert Hoover. Frederick also proposed a solution for the Depression based on the notion of making a lot more stuff. But her recommended engine for growth was not an externally, or even physically, determined end of life for products. Frederick astutely proposed consciously promoting people's love of changing fashions. (Frederick, herself a soon-to-obsolesce product of her times, restricted almost all her comments to topics concerning women of the era, but they most certainly applied more broadly then, and still do.) As she put it, "The same thrill that women have always had over new clothes, women are now also obtaining over replacement, changes, reconstruction, new colors and forms in all types of merchandise." So, instead of getting a new dress, or iron (or iPad) because your old one was recalled by the government, or because it broke and was designed to be unfixable, Frederick bypasses all that tedious regulatory or physical obsolescence, and proposes "progressive obsolescence," where you simply get a new dress or iron or iPad for the thrill of it.

It's important to note that London and Frederick were not entirely dastardly "Waste Makers."[15] They were living in a country that was seized by a crippling depression and simultaneously enthralled by the promise of "business efficiency," and where the full impacts of the "wheels of industry" on human lives and natural resources were not yet totally apparent. But to those living and working and designing today, when those impacts have become abundantly clear, it is inexcusable to hide behind design when truly assessing a product, inside and out. Just because an Apple product is beautiful, or new, or "good enough to lick,"[16] in the words of Steve Jobs, does not mean it is good.

A truly "good" design is more than lickable. As Dieter Rams outlined in the 1970s, "good design is honest," "long-lasting," and "environmentally friendly." Today more than ever, Mrs. (as well as Mr., Ms., and Mx.) Consumer needs a way to satisfy a "Love of Change," and more important, the need to make a phone call, in a way that does not harm the environment, the people making the phone, and the people who are (hopefully) recapturing the materials in it. They need a phone that is durable, easily repairable, upgradable, made with nontoxic materials according to fair labor practices, and which at the end of its (long) life is truly recyclable.

This seems like a tall or impossible order, but there are designers working on phones such as this. One important pioneer is called Fairphone: a smartphone deliberately designed to have less negative social and environmental impacts. It pitches itself as easy to repair, offers transparent repair services and instructions, and is constructed out of responsibly sourced, conflict-free, and recycled materials. The newest version, Fairphone 3, released in September 2019, already has a full repair report by iFixit that gives it a score of 10/10 for repairability.[17] In comparison, most iPhones get a 6/10 from iFixit for repairability often because of easily breakable screens, the use of glue inside the machine, the lack of repair guides or documentation, the use of proprietary screws, and other fun design decisions.

Fairphone does not yet produce a tablet, so Michael is out of luck in terms of avoiding scraping shards of glue. And Fairphone is just one small company in a very crowded landscape of technology and gadget manufacturers. Apple, too, is just one company, but a behemoth with the power to shape the market. If a company like Apple began to reconceive its design process to consider not just aesthetics but also the full life cycle—and to design for real revenue from modularity, service, and upgrade, along with real wages for the people who could provide those repair services, then the overdue journey to truly "good" digital products might really begin.

The Christmas Reindeer and the "Fake Nice" Lamp: Materials and Parts, Especially Plastic

One December, Claire G. brought us her little stuffed reindeer to fix. He was about nine inches tall to the top of his antlers, had a light-up nose, and he was supposed to move his legs and make music. (I bet you can guess the song.) The reindeer had seen many Christmases in Claire's house, and she was quite fond of him. She brought him to one of our holiday pop-ups, and in the spirit of the season, we really wanted to fix him for her at a reasonable price. But when we opened the little guy up and found a cracked plastic gear, we groaned.

Inside Claire's reindeer's stuffed chest cavity, a set of plastic gears connected to a small motor. One of these gears was split and couldn't grab the neighboring cog, so the deer's legs didn't move. We groaned when we discovered this because plastic is, very simply, a pain in the butt to fix. It's hard to glue, and once compromised—cracked, scratched, nicked—it's very hard to do anything useful with it at all. If you've got a plastic finish on something, you can, maybe, paint it or touch it up. But when plastic is used on component parts that take any stress, especially moving parts, it can mean that one small break makes the entire object useless.

Now, perhaps you don't consider stuffed reindeers to be items of the highest utility—that's okay, it was Claire's and she loved it. But there are lots of other items that have this problem, and we confronted them over and over again in our repair shops. In fact, one of the items that launched our whole repair shop endeavor was what I call a "fake nice" desk lamp. I purchased it (I think) at a Kmart years ago. It's brushed silver in color, and it resembles a high-quality swivel neck desk lamp. But it had a plastic part right in the swiveling part of the neck—exactly where all the stress was concentrated, the point with the largest range of motion. Not surprisingly, the lamp broke right at that plastic piece, and the head now dangles grotesquely from the arm. It's difficult to take this part out, even if you could find or make a replacement, because it is riveted in place, not screwed. This is why I call the lamp "fake nice." It looked good, but it was designed to fail, because of the choice of materials and the near impossibility of replacing its parts.

You might ask, why not glue the little reindeer cog? Or, couldn't a well-placed screw have saved the lamp? Well, not usually. We have used countless different types of glue on plastic, as well as fillers, heat treatments, epoxies, acrylics, resins. Some of them work, especially if you are just building up a little missing piece or filling a crack—something decorative. But when you put a plastic piece under the stress of motion and pressure, glue does not cut it. It crumbles, it gets brittle and breaks, and most important, it doesn't bond. It is sometimes possible to find adhesives that will work with a particular plastic. For example, we have used glue to reattach metal legs to a molded plastic 1960s style chair; the manufacturer kindly provided a repair kit with the correct adhesive and parts. But the vast majority of manufacturers don't supply handy kits with their plastic products, and the number of different plastics and glues out there is mind-boggling.

A lot of what we did in our repair shops, in addition to obvious breaks, was maintenance—cleaning out goop, refreshing finishes. Again, plastic is not an easy material to work with. Plastic looks good new, and it's relatively easy to clean—up to a point. Once the finish is compromised, however, it is much harder to renew than other materials. Wood, for example, can be sanded, filled, stained, waxed, sealed, or painted. Metal can be repainted, or brushed—although it's true that once dented it's not easy to un-dent. Textiles can be darned, overdyed, stitched, or patched. Plastic can't take most of these techniques; it doesn't even take paint easily.

Now, you might say that there are lots of high-tech ways to solve these problems—and for some of them there are. We could, for example, have 3-D-printed a new part for the reindeer's heart. But our aim was to provide our customers with convenient, quality, affordable repairs: we needed to be able to diagnose and fix each item quickly and easily. The amount of time it would take to scan the old part, adjust the drawing as needed, and print the new part would make the cost prohibitive. The 3-D printing would be especially time consuming in the case of my lamp, where the broken part is half missing and the other half of it is stuck in the neck of the lamp: there is nothing to scan, so we'd have to re-create it from scratch. While 3-D printing is great technology, until manufacturers make all the parts drawings for their products easily available—or just plain make the parts available—it's not really practical, especially since each repair is different. It's not as if we get a parade of reindeer, each with exactly the same cog broken in the same way. There are some interesting products out there, like Sugru, a moldable puttylike substance designed to address some of the challenges of plastic repair. But given the wide variety of plastics, and paints, and putties, and adhesives, it is often hit or miss—and it shows in the numbers.

Of the roughly 2,500 items we fixed over the years, we had a repair success rate of about 85 percent. Of the 15 percent "repair fails," nearly 70 percent involved either poor material choices (usually plastic), the nonavailability of parts, or both. If you prefer the prose version of this statistic, a short look over our database of repairs reveals a depressing litany of moments when we were stymied by plastic, unable to complete the fix, and forced to send the object back to the customer, most likely to be consigned to the trash. Here is a sample of the ways plastic crops up in our database, where we track what the customer tells us, and we record the fixer's steps and success (or not). You can hear the frustration:

From the customers:
- juice press: fix deformation of plastic
- kid's toy dog: wobbly—plastic part broken
- CD player: plastic pieces are broken
- alarm clock: always reads open, doesn't play; plastic hinge broken
- Honeywell fan: won't sit in stand because broken plastic; please figure out how to fix

From the fixers:
- barometer: couldn't fix, broken plastic; all rusted and screw missing
- short standing lamp, cream lamp shade: plastic socket broke, need to order new
- B&D blender: plastic gear shattered but replacement part unavailable
- sewing machine: no repair—deteriorated plastic clasp for wind/sew button
- CD player: no repair; CDs removed, broken plastic mechanism inside (would cost $100 to repair)
- Aiwa stereo: no repair—cracked plastic part
- meat grinder: bad plastic gear inside, please recycle
- oscillating fan: starts okay; broken plastic thing inside, will not oscillate again
- space heater: melted plastic switch inside, can't fix, not safe

We often think of the problems with plastics as a question of single-use items—water bottles and grocery bags and picnic forks. These items are designed to be used once, and discarded, and the problems inherent in this system are enormous. But my journey into the entrails of Claire's reindeer, plus the hundreds of other little plastic parts we've fought with over the past six years, has taught me that plastic components make many nonplastic objects disposable. The basic design of the reindeer—and my lamp, and many of the thousands of objects in our database—are fundamentally compromised by the incorporation of plastic into designs in a way it should never have been used.

That's why we groaned when we saw Claire's little reindeer's broken plastic cog during his open-heart surgery. We knew that we were up against a tough fix. We did manage to epoxy the gear. I even did a tiny little splice—I epoxied a tiny piece of metal across the crack, to create a sort of a splint. I've done that several times—sometimes drilling two tiny holes with a Dremel so that I could wire a broken plastic piece and give the adhesive a fighting chance. We managed to get the patched gear into the reindeer. (It took two tries.) We restuffed him and stitched him up, and we laughed and maybe even cried a little bit when he danced and sang: a little Christmas miracle. Though, to be honest, I must admit that I am not sure how long his new heart will last. It wasn't what we call a good fix—when we send an object out confident that it is as good as or even better than it was to begin with—the kind of fix we can often achieve with well-designed objects made with wood, or metal, or even plastic used in the right way.

I understand that plastic is part of our world today, and sometimes it can be an amazing, and amazingly useful, material. But it is also a problem, especially when it compromises the integrity of a much larger object. In *Cradle to Cradle*, McDonough and Braungart use the term "monstrous hybrid" to describe objects like the reindeer or my "fake nice" lamp—things where poor material choices for one component or part can compromise an entire object. Monstrous hybrids are items that, in addition to often being hard to fix, cannot be broken down into their component parts for reuse or to biodegrade and feed another "biological nutrient" cycle. As an example, the authors describe a standard book jacket that "is not really paper, but an amalgam of materials—wood pulp, polymers, and coatings, as well as inks, heavy metals, and halogenated hydrocarbons. It cannot be safely composted, and if it is burned, it produces dioxins, some of the most dangerous cancer-causing materials ever created by humans." God knows what the little reindeer would do to us if it ever fell into the Christmas fire.

But McDonough and Braungart do not dismiss all high-tech materials and expect everyone to read books printed on bamboo or recycled toilet paper. They argue, not just with their words but also with the physical book they designed, which is printed on a type of plastic, that certain plastics *can* be valuable "technical nutrients," that is to say, a material that can be endlessly recycled and upcycled, without degrading in quality, and that "can be designed with their future life foremost in mind, rather than as an awkward afterthought." Plastic on its own isn't the only problem. And "green" or "renewable" materials aren't the only solution. It's a question of considering the full life cycle of the book, or the lamp, or even the reindeer. In the longer term, that means designing objects in such a way and with materials that can be reclaimed. In the shorter term, it means making it possible, and even easy, to fix them—and that includes making parts available.

The Part about Parts

You know when a villain enters in a really amateurish play, and scary music swells? Well, cue that music now, because: enter the Nespresso coffee machine. If the reindeer felt like a cute object unfairly cut short by a faulty heart design, and the iPad felt like a manipulative little conniver, the Nespresso (and, to be fair, a lot of other kitchen appliances, especially toaster ovens) seems to be diabolically designed to tick all the boxes of *not* "good stuff."

The Nespresso was shiny, and looked quite nice, but we couldn't even get it open. It was shut tight with proprietary screws (much like an iPhone—aha!) so that we couldn't open it to even begin the diagnosis. Nespresso does offer repair services if you dig deep enough on its website or wait on hold long enough, and it will give you a loaner machine while repairing yours. But the design of the object itself very clearly says "do not enter, do not fix." One iFixit repair guide recommends "melting a Bic pen into the shape of the screw" to access the innards of the machine; we gamely tried this technique, with unsurprisingly mixed results.[18]

Whenever we encountered proprietary screws, we basically knew it was game over. Logically, objects that are made not to be opened are also usually very hard to get parts for. And while the Nespresso happened to catch the brunt of our ire, it's not at all an outlier. Twenty percent of the items we received over the years were appliances, but 52 percent of our repair fails were in this category. Of the almost six hundred appliances we tackled, 16 percent ended in a note on the repair tag: "parts unavailable," usually with a frowny face. Parts used to be more widely available.[19] And there are still some companies that make parts available: KitchenAid is notably helpful, as are certain vacuum manufacturers. As a result, our success rate on KitchenAid products was 78 percent, as compared to the 65 percent overall rate for appliances.

It seems very basic. Why not make parts available, so that people can fix their coffee machines or toaster ovens? The answer, of course, comes back to the same old, same old: the businesses selling these machines have no incentive to make parts available. They have one revenue stream: new coffee machines (and now, of course, disposable pods to fill them with). Repair services have become a luxury, a bonus for high-end products, or a reward for people who have time to wait on hold for hours at a time—rather than a normal, everyday part of life, and business. Companies like Nespresso and Apple prefer to make screws proprietary so that they can limit repairs to licensed service providers—all fine and good. But if the providers are few and far between, and the product is not designed to be fixed, the result is not quality control but simply an object that winds up in the trash because it's too hard to get it fixed.

The economics of repair used to be very different. Fifty years ago, when more items were made in the same country where they might be fixed, the relative labor costs were not so disparate. Today, however, when a manufacturer might be paid three dollars per hour to make a coffee machine in China or India, when raw materials and fuel for shipping are cheap, and a fixer in the States requires at least minimum wage, and hopefully more, it's easy to see how making new cheap stuff became the dominant model.[20]

It is possible, however, to imagine other models. There is a version of a coffee machine or other appliance that works more like a photocopier. Not that it copies your coffee, but that you rent the machine as opposed to own it. Not very long ago, businesses used to buy copiers. Today, they are largely rented, with service contracts. The company, not wanting to send a service person all the time, has an incentive to make a machine that runs properly, and that can be fixed in a reasonable amount of time when the fixer is sent out to look at it. Rental models have started to take hold in other industries—notably clothing, but also more recently furniture, with brands from Rent the Runway to Feather joining Ricoh and Toshiba in leasing goods to people. Why not coffee machines? It's also possible to imagine a sort of Fairphone situation—a coffee machine that can get cleaned, serviced, updated, tricked out with the latest modular bells and whistles.

It should be said that it's also possible to simply use a French press or Italian stovetop coffee maker, and forgo the bells and whistles. Once you have seen the moldy inside of a few of these big fancy machines, as I did many times at the shop, you might go for something simpler, too. But if you really want a machine, an upgradable model could work— especially as "things" get "smarter" all the time. The road of continuing to make unrepairable, shoddy stuff *and* connecting it all to the internet of things is an all-new level of waste that makes me shudder.

As companies develop alternative business models that include repair and upgrade, or rental, it's a fair bet that, unfortunately, a few of them will develop a service program and then design things to break so that they need to be fixed. Occasional shoddy workmanship and cut-rate business dealings are always going to be a part (though hopefully a small percentage) of the stuff landscape. But well-made products do exist, and as we develop these alternate revenue streams from repair, rental, service, and upgrade, the incentive for manufacturers and retailers to make good things will increase. So, having spent some time examining a lot of things that aren't good, it's important to clearly articulate how to identify actual good stuff.

The Birthing Stool

I don't want to spend this whole chapter complaining about diabolical iPads or moldy and unnecessary coffee machines. I haven't even mentioned the Frigidaire toaster oven that was consigned to the trash just because one heating element was not available. Perhaps I was just traumatized by all the repair fails that felt avoidable, forced upon us by seemingly careless or even malicious designers and manufacturers. Because we did fix a lot of things that were really *good*, for exactly the reasons we couldn't fix others: they were well and fairly made with good materials, and designed for a long life.

One item, a bit older than a Fairphone, illustrates this definition in the extreme. Annie B. brought her antique birthing stool to our Brooklyn location one cold spring day, hoping that we could fix the chair and replace the missing leg. The stool was very old, made of a beautiful hardwood. Not knowing what it was, we labeled it "camp stool" when Annie checked it in, with the rather laconic but expressive instruction: rebuild.

Michael put the three-legged stool back together, and in the course of conversations with Annie about the price (we had to make a special trip to get a piece of oak for the leg, and needed to check with her about the added cost), we learned that the camp stool was in fact a birthing stool, inherited from her grandmother. When we told Annie we were curious about the stool, she asked her mother, who emailed with the following:

That chair has an interesting family history. It is a birthing chair from Spain. Apparently, the woman in labor hangs on for dear life to the handles on either side while gritting her teeth and breathing at the same time. This chair and the two Spanish sideboard chests in your dining room, *and* the carved Spanish chest in your living room were all in Baba's warehouse which at the time was located where the ill-fated Twin Towers came to be built. They were part of a large shipment of Spanish furniture Baba had received at his freight forwarding business, and he bought them for us and gave them to us for our house on Maryknoll Avenue. So now you know. . . . XO Mom

p.s. There are stories behind the other chairs repaired as well which you may not know. . . . So glad you are caring for them.

The chair was, in a deep way, good stuff: an object that helped build and connect a family, and that in turn, was respected and passed down. It was a pleasure to work on: the solidity of it, the beauty of the wood grain, the unique graceful shape of each piece. Michael crafted a new leg out of the oak piece he bought, and I stained it to match. You could almost feel the history in the chair, and while Annie's mother's email gave us the details, the richness and beauty of the piece itself spoke silently of the work it had done for Annie's family over the years, in the past as a helpmeet in bringing children into the world, today as a reminder of that history.

I'm not saying that every toaster oven needs to achieve the beauty and grace of an antique birthing stool, but it's an extreme example of a point that can apply even to humbler items. A well-made object, with well-chosen materials and careful thought behind it, is a pleasure to fix and can last for a very long time. And caring for it can also be a source of revenue for someone. We charged Annie $150 to fix her birthing stool. God knows how much it cost in the first place, a hundred years ago in

Spain. But it was worth it to her to fix it, even though she didn't use it for birthing. How does this calculus change when we look at things that we want to keep that are not antiques, or obviously sentimental? That is a question that brings us to the tricky issue of price.

A new coffee machine can cost anywhere from $25 to $600. It's an uncomfortable fact that if we want to start making, using, and fixing good stuff, we might have to pay a bit more for it in the first place. In contrast to the Nespresso, which we couldn't even open, we charged $140 to fix a Krups machine that costs at least $350 new. To state the obvious, if you want a repairable, high-quality coffee maker (or toaster, or vacuum, or probably, birthing stool) you need to fork over a bit more money up front. This raises the question of access. Many people, including me, can't or won't buy $350 coffee machines, which can get us stuck in a vicious cycle of cheap unfixable stuff that needs to be replaced all the time by more cheap, unfixable stuff. This is a problem for several reasons. It reinforces the outdated notion that sustainability is something that is only for the wealthy. Companies used to address this problem with layaway plans—a way to have and use things while paying for them over time. Rental models can, sometimes, have a similar result of lowering up-front payments. In the long run, of course, buying high-quality items can be more cost effective. Buying three crappy coffee machines is more expensive than buying one good one. But that doesn't mean much to the person who doesn't have $350 on hand.

The uncomfortable truth is that quality, repairable, well-designed, and *good* stuff is often more expensive. Underlying this are two harsh realities: the companies who design and manufacture our stuff are not paying the full price of the environmental harms they may be causing; and the people who actually *make* our stuff with their hands are not being paid nearly enough. So, new stuff is often cheap, but good new stuff is generally speaking, not. How do we get manufacturers—and consumers—to pay the true cost of their goods?

At some point, we come up against the role of government policies, or as McDonough and Braungart call it, regulation. They are not big fans of regulation, arguing that truly good design can not only meet but even exceed regulatory stipulations by creating products that are not just "less bad," but actively beneficial. Their argument is not convincing, however, when you look at the reality of the global stuff landscape today. A designer might be convinced, purely on the merits of the resulting product, to adopt a cradle-to-cradle approach. But most companies are still consistently tempted to cut costs by searching for a place to make the product at the lowest possible hourly wage, with the cheapest possible parts.

The only way out of this pattern seems to be national and international standards, especially for labor. Some pessimists argue that these types of standards are impossible. Nations exist around the world with large populations that are hungry for work, and global corporations exist around the world with the capacity and desire to make lots of stuff. How could we prevent the manufacturing jobs from going to the lowest bidder? Well, we have laws in the United States that prevent food that is rotten or unhealthy from being sold or served. Why should we sell stuff that is made by people working in rotten or unhealthy conditions, or that does not meet certain basic quality standards? Currently, international labor standards are complex, and generally patchy and poorly enforced, and the result can be seen in many of the things we buy and use. Every day in our shops, we were physically cognizant of the work that went into making every item we fixed, and the person far away who made them. We were squeezed for time on each repair, trying to match an impossibly low hourly wage overseas while trying to pay our fixers enough to make rent here in New York. The fact of the matter is that until people all over the world are paid more fairly, it will be very hard to pay your rent in the United States by fixing things.

While this problem can feel impossibly huge, it is possible to take action on many levels. We can advocate for treaties and international standards that protect workers around the world. We can advocate for local incentives that make repair more financially feasible. In 2017, Sweden instituted a significant tax break for repair providers, which would cut the cost of repairs for items like shoes, clothing, and bicycles.[21] If New York State did something like this—or even just exempted repair providers from the 8 percent state sales tax—our shops' extremely slim profit margins would have doubled at least. And while we fight for smart policies, we can also start changing the way we shop, right now.

It can be daunting to try to find ethically produced products, but we have some experience to draw from. We're used to wading through potentially misleading labels on food and beauty products: products vaguely called "green" or "natural" are often far from good. It's becoming similarly confusing in terms of labor standards and ethical production of our durable goods as well. Some labels come from reputable third-party organizations; Fair Trade USA, for example, works with third-party auditors to implement regular, detailed evaluations of supply chain actors for thousands of brands. Some are more nebulous, from "voluntary membership" organizations that are funded by the companies they rate. Nonetheless, if you can find certification from third parties, it's one way to at least begin to identify responsible corporate actors for social and environmental impact.

Ensuring fair trade is complicated. As in any system, there are those who find ways to take advantage, so in some instances the benefits may not trickle down to the workers as intended. That is why some labels have been criticized by some as "marketing malarkey," claiming that while the model may have good intentions, it does not always work. One report famously shared an example of a supposedly fair trade tea cooperative where the modern toilets funded with the premium were exclusively for the use of senior co-op managers. Abuses like this only serve to further demonstrate the clear need for binding treaties, smart government policies, and reliable third-party oversight. China Labor Watch, to cite just one watchdog group, reports a range of abuses from extreme hours, exposure to toxic substances and harassment, poor living conditions, lack of grievance channels—the list goes on.[22] So while the various certifications may be confusing, and at times flawed (and none yet assure repairability or availability of parts, unfortunately for those of us who try to fix them), there are many organizations that provide valuable oversight and certification. And for the average consumer, looking for reputable fair trade certifications is a better bet than just shopping blindly, or just searching for the lowest price.

Given this complicated global landscape of manufacturing, finding good new products can take a little time; from figuring out where the item was made and by whom to figuring out whether the materials are good quality, and finally, if it was designed to last and be fixed if needed. Finding goods with these characteristics also usually means spending a little more. For this reason, from a personal standpoint, it's worth making buying new stuff a rare experience. And from an environmental and social perspective, rare and more expensive is also a good thing. This probably means buying less, and less often, which may mean in turn that you can spend more when you do buy. Truly *good* stuff is a wonderful thing, and something we can all appreciate—once in a while. Luckily for all of us, there are good alternatives to new stuff all around us, if we could just find them in all the clutter.

PART II

NOT TOO MUCH

Why do we have so much?

Michael Pollan argues that "food is not just fuel. Food is about family, food is about community, food is about identity. And we nourish all those things when we eat well."[1] He also famously clarified that, despite these wonderful qualities, too much food is a problem. The availability of cheap and low-quality food calories in modern American society has helped fuel a national obesity epidemic and damaged our soil and water. Similarly, we are currently awash in low-quality cheap "stuff" calories, and the effect on our homes and planet is equally burdensome.

We know that as humans, we need stuff; we are deeply entangled with it. And we know that stuff can be a good thing, or at least that some stuff is better than other stuff. The caveat is that, as with food, there can be too much of a good thing. The surfeit of unhealthy stuff calories in our lives doesn't only create clutter, or pollution. It helps to define who we are, as individuals and as a society: our stuff tells a story. As a result of a variety of influences, both external and internal, our shared story has become one of excess and of being overwhelmed, or heedlessly consuming and exploiting; but we are beginning to find ways out of all the mess and toward a simpler narrative, a healthier "stuff culture" that tells a story of balance and joy.

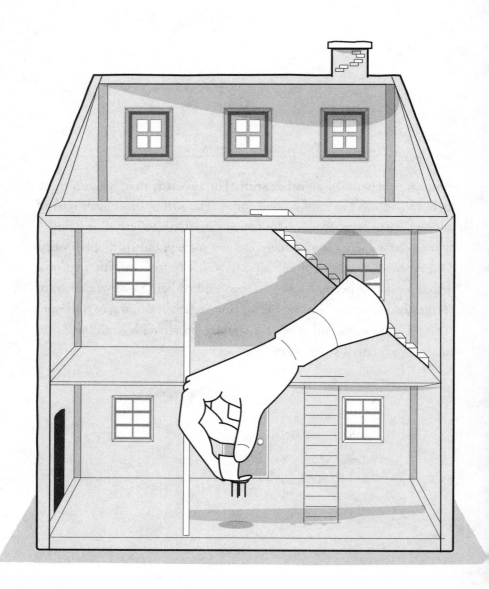

CHAPTER 3:

Our Stuff, Our Selves

It is a truth universally acknowledged that a book about stuff must be in want of a chapter on hoarders.
—Jane Austen . . . ?

Or at least I think Jane Austen wrote something like that, but I can't find the book on my crowded shelves to pull the quotation. Regardless of what Austen may have thought about it, there are *two* topics that any self-respecting stuff book must address in 2020, and those topics are hoarders and Marie Kondo. I know this because my sister, who has had her own battles with clutter, texted me recently to ask, *yr going to have a chapter on hoarders in your book, right? Kondo-ing my clothes now.* Hoarding may be a modern phenomenon, but it has deep roots. In the 1990s, psychology researcher Randy Frost began studying the condition, which he traced back to the fourth circle of hell in Dante's Inferno:

"Why do you hoard?" and the other: "Why do you waste?"
"Hoarding and squandering wasted all their light

and brought them screaming to this brawl of wraiths.
You need no words of mine to grasp their plight.[1]

Frost's work helped bring the concept of hoarding to the mainstream. The topic took hold of American popular consciousness in the early 2000s, best captured in the schadenfreude-fueled TV series *Hoarders*, which followed (and pathologized) people who are unable to get rid of anything and often live in dirty, dangerous, and incredibly cluttered environments. After a decade of being dragged through the mud of reality TV, hoarding acquired the respectability of classification as a unique disorder in the 2013 edition of the *Diagnostic and Statistical Manual of Mental Disorders*.[2] As for Marie Kondo, she exploded onto the stuff scene with her 2011 book, *The Life-Changing Magic of Tidying Up* (and a 2019 Netflix series on the same topic). Kondo's book is about how to keep a home tidy, starting by getting rid of masses of unnecessary stuff. Her refreshing blend of kindness, practical tools, and brutal honesty served as a wake-up call for millions: it's fun to see socks arranged by color, it can actually be empowering to live in a neat home, and it is encouraging to see so many Americans come to terms with how much unnecessary stuff we have—which is a lot.

It's difficult, statistically, to get inside every American's closet to calculate exactly how much excess stuff we accumulate. Many assessments of clutter are taken through proxy measurements, like the increase in space we now have to keep things in. Americans have bigger homes to fill today, almost double the square footage we had fifty years ago, and self-storage space in America now totals 2.3 billion square feet.[3] But some things you don't really need statistics to prove: it's evident to the naked eye that we've got *a lot* of stuff in this country, and we struggle to cope with it all.

So, despite my sister's hopes, this chapter isn't strictly about the horror of hoarders, or the aspirational perfection of Marie Kondo; the fetishization of tidiness and mess are just flip sides of the same coin. It's about what those shows and fads and obsessions reveal: a society where many people are not happy with what their stuff is saying. Because through our decisions (and struggles) about stuff, we build our homes around ourselves. In doing so, we create a story for and *of* ourselves—an identity—within them.

The Wheeled Bunny and the Hawk Perch

Susan B. brought us her wheeled bunny at an uptown greenmarket drop-off day. The bunny was about six inches long, fairly old, and painted red, yellow, and blue. A wheel had fallen off, and Susan was very particular about how it should go back on. We talked through the process and I could tell that she cared a lot about her bunny, and didn't want the wheel slapped on any old way. Susan's bunny was small, neat, singular. And the way she spoke about it was similarly precise; she wanted the wheel reattached so that it would still turn, even though the bunny lived on a shelf and was never played with, and she even requested an old-looking nail if possible, to match the other wheels. Curious if one object might give some insight into how our customers approached their homes, I asked Susan if she would send me pictures of her home. The images revealed a tidy apartment where the bunny would clearly be right at home: attention to detail, a love of color, a certain whimsy within a careful aesthetic.

Eileen T., on the other side of town, brought her hawk perch to our location in a thrift shop in Brooklyn. It turns out that the perch was just the tip of the iceberg—in addition, she brought us dusty chairs, half a brass bedstead, a DVD player, a candle holder, a stained-glass frame, a rosary, a brass lamp, a birdbath, a serrated knife, a sewing machine, a sign reading WELCOME TO THE NUTHOUSE, and a second hawk perch. It is very possible that you, like me at the time, do not really know what a hawk perch is. It sounds rather specific, but in fact, it was basically a couple of short lengths of two-by-four pine hinged together to make a place for a hawk to, yes, perch. It couldn't have been simpler. We fixed it, as we fixed the chairs and the bedstead (and the other half of the bedstead when she brought it in later), along with the rest of her assortment.

As the flow of broken items continued apace, it became pretty clear that Eileen's Brooklyn home must have been jam-packed with a *lot* of stuff. I didn't quite have the nerve to ask to see pictures of her home, as I had with Susan, but Eileen's belongings communicated quite eloquently that their owner had a very different style. Susan brought her bunny carefully wrapped in a towel and a bag, while Eileen would breeze into the shop with dusty chairs slung casually about her person, breathlessly promising to be right back with more. Eileen's items were loose—literally, the joints were loose—and messy, and she herself was casual about what we did to them. She was very happy with whatever we proposed, as long as it came back to her better than it had gone out. If Susan was precise and detailed about what she wanted, Eileen was fast and very relaxed.

But even without the owner's instructions, the objects themselves gave us a clue. Eileen's dusty chairs, her goofy sign, her desperately mangled bedstead, communicated an approach to the home (and perhaps to life?) that was characteristic of their owner, as did Susan's carefully maintained and polished antique toy. Neither approach was right or wrong; the objects were simply telling us, quite clearly, about each woman's home, her story, and the particular stuff culture she lived in. Those objects, and the thousands of others we fixed, had something to say.

Stuff Speaks

During my many years working as a theatrical designer, my job was to define spaces and fill them with carefully chosen objects that helped to tell a story. Many people think of scenery as background, inanimate and mute, serving only to tell us in a limited way about "location." But as any good designer or director knows, design elements are a vital part of shaping and defining how the audience understands a piece. Any play you watch has several layers to the story the audience understands. First, of course, there are the words the playwright wrote. Those words, however, may carry very different meanings depending on how the actors deliver them. And then there are multiple layers of "text" or story that can be created without any words at all, through the visual imagery created onstage, through music, through the actor's bodies, and their costumes. Good theatre exploits these many forms of meaning, layering and juxtaposing complementary (and sometimes contrasting) points of view about the same written text.

All these different forms of communication can be "read" by the audience, including the unspoken text of the visual image—of objects in space in relation to a human body. In other words, design not only supports the meaning in the text but helps create new meaning besides. The careful juxtaposition of people and things in light and space can be one of the main clues for the audience as to what a particular production is saying, and what differentiates one production from another. For example, a production of *Midsummer Night's Dream* set in a white box carries a different meaning than a production set in "traditional" Elizabethan space, or than a version set in a high school gym. The words spoken by the actors may technically be the same in each show, but the setting can help change how we understand these words.[4] And so, onstage at least, it seems that walls and things can indeed speak.

And despite their usually quiet demeanor, the things in our home speak as well. Consciously or not, we select things that help tell our real-life stories, as we understand them or want them to be understood. This idea may be most easily illustrated by clothing.

The Language of Clothing

Clothing, as any lover of Marie Kondo will know, makes up a large percentage of our stuff. The US apparel industry today is a $12 billion business, and the average American family spends $1,700 on clothes annually, more than 10 percent of our annual stuff budget.[5] In 1930, the average American woman owned only nine outfits—today that has more than tripled to thirty outfits.[6] At first glance, it might seem as though we rather sensibly own all these clothes to cover our bodies— but actually, we don't wear them. Some estimates indicate that Americans wear only 10 to 20 percent of the clothing in our closets.[7] Clearly, we accumulate clothes for reasons beyond physical coverage.

Our purposes in acquiring clothes are more complex, and are rooted in storytelling. In *Clothing: A Global History*, Robert Ross identifies the reasons humans wear clothes as Schutz, Scham, and Schmuck. In case you aren't familiar with these excellent terms, guaranteed to get a cheap laugh in a college classroom, they translate to protection, modesty, and ornament. So, yes, we do wear clothes to protect our bodies from the heat or the cold and to cover our private bits (however "private bits" are defined in a given culture). But "ornament," the last category, covers a lot, from neckties to Nikes and everything in between. What motivates us to develop and utilize such a wide variety of styles of dress is the power of clothing as language. As Ross says, "Essentially, people use clothes to make two basic statements: first, this is the sort of person I am; and secondly, this is what I am doing."[8]

These two basic statements cover a lot of ground. Our clothes can communicate our job (teacher, police officer), our task or activity du jour (biking, sleeping, gardening), our emotions (I am depressed so I am wearing my schlumpy pajamas to the store), our social groups (preppy, goth, Jets fan), our aspirations (a suit for a job interview). Sometimes our freedom to speak with our clothing is restricted (prison uniforms or school dress codes). And, as with all language, it is at times a struggle to know what we really want to say; we can even lie with our clothes. My legendary costume design teacher in grad school always recommended that if we were not feeling up to a task, we should tie a red ribbon around our neck to project strength we didn't really feel. Maybe Donald Trump took her class, too. Ross further points to the complexities of the language of clothing: "Sartorial grammars . . . have to be learnt, either as a child or as a (young) adult. This may lead to a situation of bilingualism, and potentially interesting moments of 'code switching.'"[9] Who hasn't dressed differently depending on the social group they will encounter? And who hasn't made "grammatical errors" in clothing, showing up at an event inappropriately dressed? You may use your clothes simply to say "I'm at work," or "I actually am a Jets fan." Or perhaps you agree with anthropologist Daniel Miller that we are like onions, just a series of layers with no single "true" identity at the core—in which case, clothes do at least partially make the man. In either instance, the power of clothing to "speak" is something most people can instinctively understand.

The idea of speaking or reading objects other than clothing, such as couches or hawk perches, can be a bit more of a stretch. It's likely that theatrical set designers and other people who work with stuff all day long are especially attuned to the language of things. Marie Kondo, for example, begins every tidying episode by "greeting" her client's home, sitting down on the floor and bowing her head, to hear what the space and the things in it have to say. This moment never fails to captivate her clients and the viewer. (A little careful editing and music doesn't hurt—don't forget about the power of design to create meaning!) It is Kondo's fundamental respect for the home and the objects in it that helped set her apart from so many other clutter-beaters. Kondo has her clients thank each article for its service before letting it go. She taps books to "wake them up" before sorting them. She treats everything in the home, from heirlooms to the most hopelessly overstuffed drawerful of kitchen utensils, with respect and love. In doing so, Kondo unabashedly acknowledges the role that objects play in creating our worlds, our personal narratives, and she empowers her fans to consciously rewrite their individual stories into something healthier, happier, and full of joy.

Collected Stories

Kondo's association of tidiness with joy is not new news—there is a long and rich history of people, especially Americans, supposedly linking their personal possessions with their happiness, and there is an equally long and rich history of people critiquing that association. In *The Story of Stuff,* Annie Leonard lamented our tendency to confuse our stuff with our "personal self-worth." More than a hundred years earlier, Thorstein Veblen described a theory of the "leisure class," where the possession of goods became "requisite to the complacency which we call self-respect," most conspicuously by offering a "classification of oneself as compared to one's neighbors." The desire for—and dangers of—stuff is as old as stuff itself, as amply evidenced in exhortations against materialism in many ancient texts, from the Bible to Buddhism and beyond.

What is unique to our era is our technological capacity to both stoke and fulfill this ancient and perhaps very normal desire for stuff. This capacity of advertising and production at a massive scale took off after World War II, but started at least as early as the late nineteenth century, and arguably much earlier. In colonial America, fashion plates from France allowed people to copy the latest styles, albeit several months late. Today, you can scroll through a hundred images on your phone while you wait for your computer to start. And as the exposure and the desire grow, our capacity to satisfy those desires, with ever cheaper and more numerous objects, grows as well: from the first spinning jenny to today's massive manufacturing capabilities. As with food, the desire may be natural. What is not natural, or at least is not serving us well, is our capacity to make ever more, and the erosion of cultural taboos or limits to overconsumption.

For just as our desires are shaped by our perceptions of what our peers do, the rules of how we consume are governed by our culture, meaning the cumulative habits of a given group of people. Our friend Michael Pollan refers to food culture as, "the various social structures that surround and steady our eating, institutions like the family dinner, for example, or taboos on snacking between meals and eating alone."[10] Pollan has described the erosion of this culture and its replacement with an anxiety-ridden and ever-shifting terrain of food fads and fear-induced whiplash dietary changes. He argues that Americans don't know *what* to eat, for a few reasons: We are a nation with multiple cultural origins, so we do not have one dominant traditional food culture. We are individualistic, so are prone to follow food fads or "choose your own adventure" eating. And our already fragmented food culture has been further weakened by heavily processed and marketed "foodlike" products pushed by a powerful industry. As a result, we don't have a single strong, nutritious, and joyful way of eating—so we piece together a hodgepodge of diets and regimens, or we simply wind up eating out of the carton in front of the fridge. Predating this rather unsuccessful pattern, and still alive in many parts of the world, are long-standing food cultures—traditional diets and ways and places for eating that worked for centuries to keep people alive and healthy, to unify families, to welcome guests, and to connect human beings with the land that feeds them.

Like food, stuff comes from the earth, it's a fundamental necessity for our species, and we have evolved a rich culture of making, using, and expressing ourselves through it. So, adapting Pollan's definition of food culture works for stuff culture as well: the various social structures that surround and steady our homes, habits like making the bed or spring cleaning, for example, or taboos on throwing perfectly good items away. This last bit of a traditional stuff culture seems to still be alive and kicking. I can't tell you how many customers at our repair shops came in anxious and stressed because they felt they were going to have to toss something that was "perfectly good" except for one small break. Even in our consumer republic, there is still a taboo against this type of waste, for both food and stuff.

The food analogy extends further. Our current American food culture, as has been amply demonstrated, contributes to a nationwide obesity epidemic, plus a variety of other health problems. Approximately one third of adults and up to 20 percent of children and adolescents in the United States are obese.[11] We have high rates of heart disease, diabetes, bad teeth, and all sorts of other problems that are directly linked to our "Western diet," which is characterized by big portions, and "lots of processed foods and meats, lots of added fat and sugar, lots of everything except fruits, vegetables, and whole grains."[12] Most modern Americans consume a surfeit of unhealthy or empty calories that pad our bellies and clog our arteries with fat. The production of these unhealthy foods clogs our waterways and contaminates our soil with pesticides and fertilizers. The impacts of our unhealthy diets don't stop there: American agriculture was responsible for 8.6 percent of total GHG in 2016, and almost half of hired agricultural laborers lack basic rights.[13] The link between bad food and health—and increasingly, between bad food culture and a host of other ills—is well established. If you are reading this book and have turned on the TV in the past decade, chances are you have tuned in to the impacts of food on your body, your health, and your planet.

Just as our food culture starts in the home with the family, so does our stuff culture. At our repair shop tents, we always had a box of buttons out on display. Visitors often approached our stand, drawn by the button box. It's pretty, and it keeps the kids busy while their parents drop off a lamp, or stop to talk. (You just have to make sure the smaller kids don't eat the buttons.) In addition to kid distraction, however, the button box seemed to spark memories. People run their fingers through the buttons, they smile at the satisfying *click-click*, and they invariably tell us about a grandmother or aunt who had a button box they liked to play with as a kid.

A button box is one small physical manifestation of a certain stuff culture—equivalent, perhaps, to a windowsill herb garden in a dedicated cook's kitchen. A button box implies that things will break, and that it's worth it to be prepared to fix them. And, of course, button boxes are becoming a thing of the past. I asked the students in my first-year seminar this semester, a class called Things and Stuff, how many of them had brought a sewing kit to college. The answer was five out of sixteen. Pretty low, but not bad, actually. I asked how many of them had used it—zero. Most of the visitors to our repair shops fondly remembered their grandmother's button boxes, several of them offered to donate their buttons to us, but precious few mentioned having or using their own box. A button box has become an anachronism for many people, a remnant of the past.

Stuff culture extends beyond buttons, of course. It includes everything about how we make, and shop, and use, and maintain, and discard our stuff. If the impacts of our food culture are clearly evident on our bodies, then the impacts of our stuff culture are clearly visible in our homes. And just as our food culture and practices also impact the planet, the impacts of our stuff culture extend well beyond our homes, affecting the communities where our stuff is made, and the environment.

Susan and Eileen gave us a glimpse into their homes and into their personal stuff culture through the objects they brought us, as did every other customer. Some of them, like Susan, seemed to have found a balance, a sense of satisfaction with their homes. These people often came to us with very specific items, like the wheeled bunny, that they wanted us to work on. One couple came all the way downtown to bring us one candle snuffer—the bell had broken off the handle. Their dedication to their candle snuffer, and the little ritual that it represented, was touching. Keeping that candle snuffer going was worth two trips (drop-off and pickup), and twenty-five dollars. Eileen's tsunami of dusty cracked chairs and loose portions of bedsteads indicated a totally different way of living. And then there were the customers who were not as in control of their environments as Susan or the candle-snuffing couple might be, but were not quite so freewheeling as Eileen. These people, in the middle, seemed to be striving for some sense of control, some capacity to keep on top of it all. Parents with small children often seemed to fall into this category, hoping to keep the home under control while still feeding and, presumably, nurturing the kids who hopped and pulled at their arms during drop-off, only momentarily pacified by rummaging through the button box.

These variations seem to be reflected in our popular stuff culture as well. Shows like *Hoarders* fetishize and pathologize the excess of the Eileens of the world. People who can't keep control of what they have and who are sometimes literally crushed by their stuff somehow tickle the fancy of the rest of us, perhaps making us feel better about our own "normal" homes, perhaps messy but at least free of cat carcasses. At the other end of the spectrum, makeover shows like Kondo's make order and beauty feel totally achievable, transforming cluttered or drab homes into places where Susan's bunny would feel right at home, and, on the way, creating a new narrative for their owners.

By learning to see our stuff not as passive, voiceless objects but as an active, contributing part of the story, we can consciously use our stuff to change the meaning of the tales we live. In our homes, we each design a real-life theatre set around ourselves, and we act out our lives on our little stage every day. We may be living a narrative of clutter or hoarding but want to shift to one of tidiness and joy. Or we may have an apartment that looks perfectly good, but where the practices of making our clothes and furniture are toxic to people and the planet alike. By learning how our stuff can shape our world, onstage and off, we can begin to design and live a better story, individually and collectively.

CHAPTER 4:

The Global Conspiracy to Clutter Your Home

Either we have to grow less or we have to grow very differently.
—Juliet Schor

One chilly April day, Carrie P. brought her IKEA lamp and lampshade to our tent at the 115th Street Greenmarket, just outside Columbia University in Manhattan, carefully wrapped and placed in a canvas tote. The lamp was small, a black metal table lamp about ten inches high with a cube-shaped Japanese-style crinkled paper shade. As they tend to do, the original paper shade had gotten torn, and Carrie had taken the time to find a replacement shade that was about the right size. Unfortunately, the new shade (though it was also from IKEA) didn't fit the lamp; the connection point at the top wasn't compatible. As with Karen and the shower radios, Carrie held on to her broken lamp for more than a year until she happened upon our service. Her attachment to her little lamp overrode rational economics: she paid us more to fix it than she would have for a new lamp. Carrie's lamp offers us an opportunity to ask, not why did she hold on to it, but why was it so difficult for her to get it fixed?

Like all IKEA products, the lamp had a name, although Carrie didn't remember it. The lamp was no longer sold by IKEA, but on a site called Ikeahackers.net, I found a picture of what seemed to be the same lamp, though altered: it's called a Gusle. In 2006, someone hacked their Gusle lamp by installing nudie stamps behind the paper of the shade: the risqué postage is only revealed when the Gusle is lit. (Hacking, or modifying IKEA products is a thing, with multiple sites and Pinterest boards devoted to all kinds of projects from naughty backlit postage stamp lamps to totally reconfigured kitchen cabinet sets turned into home offices.) Carrie came looking to us for a relatively simple hack—a way to make the new shade fit the old lamp.

Although the Gusle is not sold today, a not dissimilar lamp called Majorna currently sells for $16.99. And a comparable lampshade, the Orgel, sold for $9.99. Given these prices, Carrie could probably have bought another lamp. However, like Karen (of the shower radios), Carrie didn't necessarily want a new version of her old stuff. She liked the old one, she felt it fit well in her home, and she simply didn't want a new one. Indeed, she wanted the old one enough to take the trouble to buy a replacement lampshade, hold on to it when she realized it didn't fit, and then pay us to marry the two, which we were able to do for twenty dollars. But why did we have to fix the lamp? Why didn't IKEA fix it, and pocket the twenty?

IKEA is a big, big company—the kind of global player that not only responds to trends but can drive them, too—and over the past half century it has played a significant role in shaping our current habits around home furnishing. IKEA is also a company that prides itself on its sustainability program, calling it an "integral part of [its] growth agenda and essential for business success." And yet IKEA was unable to support Carrie in her simple decision to keep her lamp. You might ask, what's one Gusle lamp in the landfill, more or less? The whole thing probably weighs less than two pounds. It's true, the lamp was small. But, as with

Andy's iPad, the problem doesn't lie only in filling our landfills with Gusles: the real environmental cost is the energy and waste we create in making and buying a new one.

Despite these environmental costs, however, the monetary cost remains so low that it is often cheaper in the United States to buy a new lamp than to fix the old one. This strange state of affairs, which we have become inured to, is because the true costs of the new lamp— in resources extracted to make it, in shipping it, in waste generated in manufacturing, and in social impacts of producing it at low wages—are not covered by the $16.99 (plus $9.99 for the shade) price tag. Those "externalities" are covered, though unequally, by all of us in the form of rising seas, resource depletion, habitat degradation, and global social inequity.[1] That one little lamp is connected to a really big mess.

But if making new stuff is the problem, what does it matter whether IKEA fixes Carrie's lamp, instead of me? Can't IKEA just stick to what it does best but do it more sustainably—sell lamps made of bamboo or mashed-up corn or reclaimed Swedish meatballs? Carrie's Gusle will ultimately show us that, until companies like IKEA begin to see multiple sources of revenue in their products *beyond the first purchase*, a truly healthier relationship with our stuff—as a society and as individuals— will remain elusive.

Small Lamp, Big System

We fixed more than four hundred lamps over the years of our pop-ups. This chapter could have been written about any number of them, and any number of manufacturers or retailers. But IKEA is one of the largest designers, manufacturers, and retailers of home furnishings in the world, and it took a leading role in shaping the current system that produced most of those lamps. IKEA is just one example of how the global system typically operates, but it's also a leader in the industry and has been able to drive change in the past—for better and for worse. IKEA is also taking very public steps to go green. In this, too, it has an opportunity to lead, either in greenwashing, or in true change for a truly global system.

You probably know this already, but just in case you want to be reminded of the astounding scale at which global industry operates, here goes; there are more than four hundred IKEA stores around the world, with upwards of $40 billion in global sales in 2018, and more than $4 billion in profit. IKEA has sold more than two Swedish meatballs for every man woman and child on earth today. IKEA's four-hundred-plus stores have an average size of 320,000 square feet per store, larger than five football fields—all stuffed with charming and accessible furniture and liberally sprinkled with umlauts. The stores are filled with all kinds of stuff made by over one thousand suppliers in fifty-one countries, and connected by an enormous infrastructure of shipping and transport. This massive machine is driven by a workforce of 149,000 direct IKEA employees worldwide, and tens of thousands more employees of third-party manufacturers making all the stuff.[2] The machine serves up products arrayed in beautiful catalogs, efficient websites, and attractive store displays. And the machine's engine is fueled by all of us: looking, touching, clicking, and buying. This vast system makes it very, very easy to get almost anything you want for your home at a low price, including a Gusle-style lamp for $16.99.

IKEA's mission is to "create a better everyday life for the many people." The vision is realized in a product line of some ten thousand objects, all created through a process of "democratic design, a conscious effort to balance form, function, quality, low price, and sustainability." There is, however, tension in this democracy; as any designer knows, the seamless marriage of form and function is not always easy to achieve, and quality, price, and sustainability are always squabbling among themselves. We feel this tension, too, when we shop there. We know at some level that it doesn't make sense for all this stuff to be so cheap, but it looks good, it feels good to buy it, and actually, IKEA design is generally excellent from an aesthetic point of view.

The concept of "democratic design" started appearing in IKEA promotional materials in 2013. But even before the label was created, many of the elements were central goals since the company's first days. In the early years of the IKEA design democracy, before sustainability was even a minor faction, price was the dominant party. In the early 1950s, IKEA was a rapidly growing company whose founder, Ingvar Kamprad, succinctly flat-packed his original aims: "My interest at first was purely commercial: selling as much decent furniture as I could as cheaply as possible."[3]

In maintaining low prices, one of Kamprad and IKEA's early tactics, and arguably the most significant in terms of the wider industry, was the focus on lowering distribution costs. Kamprad was obsessed with figuring out how to get the furniture from the manufacturer and into our living rooms while keeping the price as close to wholesale as possible. It's important to note that in these early years, IKEA's designs were not necessarily unique to the company. The products were made, usually overseas in Poland, by manufacturers who could also sell to Kamprad's competitors. So, Kamprad focused instead on ways to get the same product to his customers with a smaller markup. What made IKEA unique at first was innovation in logistical systems, especially of distribution, and the resulting low prices—not design. Innovation in form became very important, too, as the company grew, but thinking creatively about the systems of moving vast quantities of stuff across continents, through the stores and into our homes was and still is today one of the company's greatest strengths. It's also a pattern that quickly spread across the globe.

IKEA's story is, of course, the story of globalization and manufacturing in the post–World War II years, when the Western world undertook its decades-long transition to a system where brand-name retailers use third-party manufacturers, usually low-wage and overseas, to produce their goods. Materials, components, and finished products are now shipped all over the world, usually from poorer countries (where they are sourced and built) to richer countries (where they are bought, used, and discarded). IKEA, for example, works with suppliers in Eastern Europe, China and several other countries, particularly in Asia.[4] Its stores, however, tend to be located in countries like Germany, the UK and the US (though, like many big corporations, they are making a big push in China and other emerging markets). Obviously, in this model, shipping costs are a big consideration, as are labor costs in the generally higher-wage countries where things are sold. How, given this global picture, do companies like IKEA keep costs down?

Designed to Move—into the Dump

In terms of shaping this current model, one of IKEA's most notable innovations was the flat pack. We are all so accustomed now to flat packaging that we don't realize what a breakthrough of engineering and design it is that virtually all IKEA's stuff can be delivered more or less in a flat box—furniture wasn't always broken down for shipping so easily. The origin story involves Gillis Lundgren, a young draftsman who eventually went on to hold key roles at IKEA managing product lines and designing hundreds of products. Lundgren, struggling to pack up a table after photographing it for a catalog in 1956, thought, "Let's pull the legs off and put them underneath." And, so the story goes, a revolution was born.[5]

Packing things flat changes the game significantly. Items can be made farther away as shipping costs are reduced, and the labor involved in assembly is shifted from the retailer to the consumer. Why pay an employee in the United States to put a table together when you can have your customer do it instead? This innovation changed the playbook for home furnishings worldwide, helping to make IKEA the giant that is today and the flat pack a global standard.

This revolution in distribution changed not only the way home furnishings are sold and delivered but perhaps also the way we feel about our stuff. A 2017 study called "The 'IKEA Effect': When Labor Leads to Love," documents the increased value people assign to objects they assemble themselves. Researchers had subjects assemble IKEA products (along with Legos and origami), and discovered that, actually, all that wrestling with hex keys and particle board leads us to perceive our stuff as more valuable than it is. The effect is "sufficient in magnitude that consumers believe that their self-made products rival those of experts." So, paradoxically, IKEA's drive to cut costs and make us put our own darn Billy bookshelves together might, in an increasingly homogenized and mass-produced world of home furnishings, make us like the shelves *more* than if we had bought a pricier, less DIY unit.

While I don't have a Harvard Business School study to prove it (yet), my years in the repair shops lead me to believe that getting something fixed also enhances a person's estimation of an object's value. Once people have taken the trouble to bring their lamp or chair or blender down to our shop, they seem committed to following through on their investments of time, of effort, and of the original purchase price. The very act of noticing, of taking action to fix the flow of an object, seems to make people willing to invest more time and money in it. It's a kind of loss aversion, compounded by the emotional attachment to the object. This is a phenomenon IKEA and other big businesses would do well to study, for in it lie the seeds of a global economic shift: that emotional attachment represents a willingness to spend money on repair, service, and upgrade. And while I am not particularly in the business of finding more ways for large corporations to make money, I am interested in corporations finding ways to make money that don't involve making masses of new stuff.

But first, we have to ponder: Having labored so hard to assemble it that we come to love our IKEA stuff, why do we chuck so much of it out? For we do, indeed, chuck a lot of it—furniture makes up 4.6 percent of household waste in the United States.[6] Of course, that includes more than just IKEA products, but nevertheless upwards of eleven million tons of furniture are sent to landfills every year. One reason we are comfortable throwing away our furniture is that IKEA itself has taught us, explicitly and repeatedly, to do so. For decades IKEA tried mightily (and by many measures successfully) to convince people that our old stuff is not worth keeping, and that we should dump it for something new.

Advertising, Nuff Said (Almost)

One award-winning commercial from 2002, directed by Spike Jonze, is called "Unböring." In it, the camera follows a lamp as it is unplugged by a woman, removed from its spot at the window, and carried (looking over her shoulder) out to the curb. Placed unceremoniously in the wind-swept and rainy gutter, we (who, at this point in the ad, are seeing the world from the lamp's point of view) can see into the house, can see the lamp's old spot at the corner table, and—worst of all—can see the new lamp that takes its place. The lamp at the curb seems to sag, rain falls, night is coming. At this point, the frame is broken by a strange man in a trench coat, who says (in an umlaut-ish kind of accent), "Many of you feel bad for this lamp. That is because you're crazy. It has no feelings. And the new one is much better. . . ."

The purpose of this admittedly funny and well-made ad was, quite simply, to change the frequency with which people bought new stuff—and to remove the "crazy" emotional attachments to old stuff that prevented people from shopping for home furnishings at a pace which would satisfy a company that grew from less than $5 billion to

$16 billion in sales in the period from 1990 to 2005.[7] Crispin Porter + Bogusky, the creative agency behind the "Unböring" campaign, targeted the ads at Americans who "spend wildly on 'fashion' purchases, such as clothes and shoes, but who still clung to a 'till death do us part attitude' with their furniture." The agency research showed that "in one American lifetime, people had the same average number of dining room tables as they did spouses: 1.6." On average, Americans kept their sofas for eight years. Bedroom furniture lasted twice as long, sixteen to twenty years. These slow turnaround times represented, to IKEA and to the ad agency that built their campaigns, a guilt-fueled attachment to stuff, an "American furniture culture . . . founded by Puritans," that was ripe for a redesign.

Breaking this puritanical (and therefore neither stylish nor profitable) attachment to old stuff worked beautifully on the other side of the Atlantic as well. IKEA's famous "Chuck Out Your Chintz" campaign launched in 1996 and featured working and middle-class women tossing their old furniture as an act of liberation. In it, dowdy but energetic British women claim their long overdue independence by relieving their parlors of fusty couches and valances, embracing their futures in homes where the work of clever Swedish designers can more adequately reflect their new identities:

We're battling hard and we've come a long way,
in choices and status, in jobs and in pay.
But that flowery trimmage is spoiling our image,
so chuck out that chintz today!

The creator of the campaign, Naresh Ramchandani, said that he crafted the campaign "for IKEA when they were sort of fighting the forces of traditional British furniture." The campaign explicitly links 1980s-style furniture—think Laura Ashley sofas and matching drapes—with outmoded roles for women, creating a feeling that "chintz is a sort of old-fashioned idea that's holding the women of the country back." This idea—to jump on the bandwagon of 1990s British feminism in order to sell furniture—worked: "The campaign was a huge success in terms of sales, with some items selling 30 percent more after the ads aired. That's quite a big swing from one advertising campaign," Ramchandani said, adding that the ads helped IKEA "find its voice in the UK and informed their marketing and communications strategy for years to come."[8]

It makes sense. A manufacturer of new furniture should, logically, want to encourage people to buy new furniture, and do so often. But when companies realize—or are forced to face the reality—that their business practices (and our habits of supporting them) are causing serious environmental or social harm or both, they can find themselves in a bind. As with its journey to global industrial dominance, IKEA's sustainability story is indicative of larger trends.

Growth and a Greener Gusle

The move toward a greener IKEA started with both external pressures and internal changes. Externally, IKEA faced public demand and regulatory requirements to reduce toxic or damaging practices, like using particle board that off-gassed formaldehyde or wood from tropical rain forests. Internally, top management saw the writing on the wall, and began to develop policies to include environmental health as a part of the "better everyday life" the company had long claimed to be creating. IKEA appointed its first environmental manager in 1989, which led the way in 1990 to IKEA's first official environmental goal: to minimize any damage to the environment. In 2004, IKEA published its first Social and Environmental Responsibility Report. And by 2012, its sustainability reports were including sustainability in the "democratic design" model, along with the original ideals of form, function, price, and quality.

But despite these efforts to reduce harm, there is a tension between the basic business of IKEA—selling more for less—and the realities of what that truly costs. IKEA, and we, their customers, are struggling to resolve this tension. What should we do? Should we really go chuck out our chintz, or should we be "frugal," another value often cited in IKEA's materials? And, from the point of view of the purveyor, is it possible to truly pursue green practices when one's business model is built entirely on always making and selling more new stuff?

Many say it is not possible, because we live in a society built on what youth climate activist Greta Thunberg scathingly dismissed as "fairy tales" of endless expansion, and an economy built on a narrow definition of what that growth can look like. Richard Heinberg writes in *The End of Growth* that "starting with Adam Smith, the idea that continuous 'improvement' in the human condition was possible came to be generally accepted . . . gradually, however, 'improvement' and 'progress' came to mean growth in the current economic sense of the term—abstractly, an increase in gross domestic product (GDP), but in practical terms, an increase in consumption." What this means for IKEA, and even more so for publicly traded companies, is that every year, annual reports are published that must display growth—in sales, in profits, in numbers of stores built. To "succeed," to have a "healthy" economy, more stores must be built, more dollars exchanged, more lamps sold every year. For Carrie and her Gusle, what this means is that there is an entire global political and economic belief system, not to mention a massive infrastructure of manufacturing, advertising, and retail, pushing her to buy a new lamp as often as possible. Really, it's a wonder she even tried to fix the old one at all. Our single-minded obsession with growth—and the exclusion of other factors, like resource depletion, labor rights, and climate change—may sooner or later be our undoing. And it's looking an awful lot like it might be sooner. As Annie Leonard put it bluntly almost fifteen years ago in the

Story of Stuff, it's a "take-make-waste model—the economy as it is will kill the planet."

So what's a forward-thinking, sustainably minded company to do? How do you live (and do business) in a growth-based model *and* care about the planet? Is that even possible? When a company is constantly making and selling more in order to grow, are all the sustainability plans in the world just lip service? Yvon Chouinard, the founder of Patagonia, a company that is widely seen as a global leader in corporate sustainability, comes down pretty bluntly on the corporate "takers and makers": "Everyone's just greenwashing. The revolution isn't going to happen with corporations. The elephant in the room is growth. Growth is the culprit."[9]

IKEA is caught in this contradiction, like all of us. IKEA is committed to and proud of growth—in 2017 the company boasted of fourteen new stores, but achieved apparently disappointing growth of only 4 percent overall: the figure is hidden in the text, instead of booming from the graphic sections, and is acknowledged to be "lower than previous years," with a promise that 2017 taught the company "how to improve our customer focus and ability to grow."[10] Growth is still king. But IKEA also publicly committed to reducing GHG emissions. To back up this commitment, IKEA has taken serious steps; by 2016 the company had installed over 730,000 solar panels, aimed to produce 100 percent renewable energy for operations by 2020, and committed to sourcing all its cotton sustainably, to name just a few measures.

But making products more efficiently, even with less damaging materials and renewable energy, doesn't add up long-term when growth means that you are locked into always making and selling more. In *Cradle to Cradle*, McDonough and Braungart argue that the dangerous effects of our current system of production and consumption on "human and ecological health" cannot be solved by designing things that are "less bad." Simply taking and wasting less in order to make even more doesn't work, because that approach simply "works within the same system that caused the problem in the first place, merely slowing it down. . . . It presents little more than an illusion of change."

In 2016, Steve Howard, IKEA's then chief sustainability officer, spent a lot of time trying to convince people that IKEA's vision for change is not an illusion—that true change is coming, direct to your living room in a flat pack. He spoke publicly and often about the limits, and not only environmental, of the IKEA model for growth; at a *Guardian* conference in 2016, Howard remarked, "If we look at a global basis, in the West we probably hit peak oil. I'd say we've hit peak red meat, peak sugar, peak stuff . . . peak home furnishings." "Peak stuff" is a state of affairs many of us face, intimately, in our overfull closets and storage units, and that also represents a significant challenge for IKEA and other businesses that are built on the model of constantly getting us to buy more. If we've maxed out our storage and our appetites for stuff, what then? How does a company like IKEA exist? What is the new engine of economic activity?

Howard and the most recent IKEA sustainability reports argue that IKEA can continue to exist *and* move away from an emphasis on "less bad" sustainability principles by shifting to a circular model rather than a linear one. A linear system is the "take, make, waste" described by Leonard, where we extract resources, make and distribute products, use them, and then toss them. In contrast, a circular economy is one where "waste" is captured and used in other processes, like remanufacturing or upcycling. A circular system also keeps things in use as long as possible, meaning products that are designed to last longer, be recycled or reused, and be easy to care for—including repair.

IKEA has started to make some moves in this direction, prototyping systems in France, Belgium, and Japan where customers can bring old items in for recycling or resale and receive a voucher in exchange. IKEA has even begun talking about repair—a necessary but often underdeveloped part of the still-young circular economy. A recent sustainability report touts the "more than a million" spare parts provided to customers in 2018, and optimistically if somewhat vaguely refers to refurbishment and reuse: "We see big potential in this service and are exploring how to scale it globally." IKEA is starting, at least, to explore alternatives to just "chucking your chintz"—that is, alternatives to a singular notion of growth based only on selling more new stuff.

IKEA Canada recently tackled the legacy of the Spike Jonze "Unböring" campaign. A new version of the ad shows our old friend, the discarded lamp, slumped in the gutter as the rain blows, melancholy music, you remember. . . . But this time, instead of a creepy Scandinavian guy in a raincoat, the frame is broken by a cheerful pretween pulling a wagon. She rescues the lamp, and in an unapologetically syrupy montage, uses it to do her homework, make shadow puppets, and illuminate tea parties. The creepy guy reappears at the end, to tell us that we are right, this time, to feel happy for this lamp. That it's better to reuse things. Our emotional attachment to our stuff is no longer crazy—it's true, meaningful, valuable. The ad is not as funny as the original—in fact, it's rather cloying. And it's important to note that the little girl didn't find the used lamp at her local IKEA store; she found it in the gutter. But nonetheless, this ad represents a huge shift.

This shift is not only semi-absurd coming from the company that, as we have seen, spent decades and millions of ad dollars convincing us that home furnishings are nearly as disposable as toilet paper; it is also revolutionary. There is a vast post-sale market for used furniture and goods—resale in the US generates approximately $17.5 billion in annual revenues.[11] But by and large, big retailers and manufacturers have almost entirely ignored both this revenue stream and the post-sale life of their products. So, IKEA's talking about reuse and repair is, indeed, a potential game changer and a really big deal—as big, perhaps, as the flat pack.

It's a game changer because it represents a revolution in how we think about growth. What if IKEA could have captured the twenty bucks that Carrie paid me to fix her lamp? What if IKEA could make money more than once from the same lamp? What if IKEA could apply its systems and logistics and design genius toward the maintenance of the old rather than the manufacture and shipping of the new? All of a sudden, there is a way to imagine uncoupling economic growth from increased consumption. After all, the twenty dollars Carrie spent contributed to the economy—it went right into the pocket of Flora, the local New York artisan who fixed the lamp. A decrease in consumption does not have to equal recession, economic disaster, or apocalypse, if as a society and as businesses—whether at my little Fixup start-up or giants like IKEA—we start recognizing and capturing the value in the things we already have.

So, which is the real IKEA? Is the sustainability plan just greenwashing, or is it an exciting vision of a future that doesn't involve canoeing to work in Midtown? Do they want us to chuck out our chintz with abandon, or keep our Gusle and lovingly repair it for years to come, as Carrie tried to do? The answer, of course, is both—IKEA is struggling along with the rest of us, at the very least talking the talk, and if not quite yet walking the walk, then taking the first steps. In 2017, IKEA purchased TaskRabbit, a major corporate step toward making repair and service part of its core business. At the same time, however, IKEA proper is still struggling with an older vision of growth, where selling more is still the main event. This type of conflicting purpose is normal for a company— and a society—faced with the need for transformational change in order to survive. And while there are encouraging signs that the company's vision is shifting, as with all strategic shifts, the picture on the ground is not always quite the same as it is at the design meeting or the conference table. In some ways, the design for change is still, unfortunately, very much on the drawing board, but not yet in the stores or built into our stuff.

Let's take repair, for example. The company's 2016 sustainability report talks about the need to make it "easy to care for, repair, adapt, disassemble and reassemble, and recycle." The reality, at least in the New York area, is still cumbersome at best, hair-tearing-out frustrating at worst. Customers are required to take broken items to the store (okay for Carrie with her little Gusle, maybe, but what about an Ektorp sofa?) with a receipt or other proof of purchase. At the store, the item is evaluated to determine whether it can be repaired (rarely) or replaced (more often), and whether IKEA is responsible for the damage. The company talks a lot about refurbishment, and does make many parts available, although that is far from a comprehensive and user-friendly DIY repair program, much less a robust in-store option. IKEA's language about repair is right on—"easy to care for, repair, adapt"—but the experience doesn't correspond quite yet.

In order to make repair truly "easy," IKEA must embrace a revolution as profound as the flat pack. It needs to grow by charging money for fixing our broken Ektorps and reattaching Carrie's ill-fitting Gusle shade, not by selling new couches and new lamps. It needs not only to tell us on the website about Kijiji (a Canadian site that resells IKEA goods) but also capture that revenue itself, in order to be able to sell fewer new Gusles, and then charge money to fix them when they break. It needs to build the systems that make getting these things fixed as simple as it was to buy them in the first place. And it will need to consider repair in the design of each product as well. For despite the internet community of IKEA hackers, who do clever things with their IKEA products and component parts, many products are still simply too difficult to really work with properly—especially the rock-bottom items like the ubiquitous college dorm room Lack table, furniture never meant to have any sort of relationship with a tool more complicated than a wooden peg. This kind of flimsy, old-school IKEA design keeps cost low in terms of materials and shipping, but it does not make it "easy to repair," and will make it incredibly difficult to achieve the circular vision IKEA is starting to tout.

But of course, with a little creativity and the right tools, even a Lack can be fixed or altered or hacked, just as Carrie's Gusle lamp was joined with its odd partner shade. The last step in making the illusion of change real will be for IKEA and many other companies to see and hear people like Carrie (and Karen and Andy and you and me) and realize that we all do indeed want to keep the things we have, and that this impulse is not crazy or puritanical, but perfectly normal—and incredibly valuable.

Growing in Circles

IKEA, of course, is not alone. Although the company may be the poster child for disposable home goods and global, linear growth, there are many companies in a similar boat. The good news is that IKEA, and indeed several of its competitors, seems to at least have seen the writing on the wall. Over the six years since Carrie brought us her Gusle, IKEA has taken significant steps toward a new business model beyond peak stuff. The term "circular economy" has gone from being a niche idea to a $20 million investment for Blackrock in 2019. According to Accenture, the circular economy could generate $4.5 trillion of additional economic output by 2030, in a system that "will help decouple economic growth and natural resource consumption while driving greater competitiveness."[12] We're beginning to recognize that solar panels on the roof are great, but they don't really matter if a company's core business model locks it into always selling more new stuff. Here's hoping that the next revolution in consumption will be led by IKEA's growing by continuing to give "the many" what they want—which in many cases, is very simply what they already have.

PART III
MOSTLY RECLAIMED

How can we rebalance our "stuff diet"?

All but the most devoted health nuts might groan, inwardly at least, at the third part of Michael Pollan's advice regarding healthy eating: "Eat food. Not too much. *Mostly plants.*" A similar response is sometimes elicited by the third step in my recommendations for healthy stuff: Have good stuff. Not too much. *Mostly reclaimed.*

Some people are devoted thrifters, sporting old MC Hammer pants or delighting in mid-century chic, and others are committed bargain hunters, eager to pick through dusty bins in search of a gem at rhinestone prices. But others have a bit of resistance to old stuff—perhaps it's an aversion to the sometimes off-putting aroma of certain thrift stores, a fear of bedbugs, or a dread of hand-me-downs rooted in perceived sibling injustices. There are many people who, especially as they move up the economic ladder, happily ditch secondhand shopping, enjoying the status that goes with wearing the latest styles. And lots of people simply love shiny new things.

Acquiring things can provide a thrill. Even watching other people acquire things has become popular: "hauls" and "unboxing" videos abound online. These videos, often featuring and aimed at young people, show a person unpacking, touching, and recounting the joys of acquiring a huge range of products: shirts from Forever 21, Xboxes, Cheetos-inspired makeup, Nike shoes, Kinder Surprise Eggs, Dollar Tree pens, prom dresses, the newest iPhone. The vicarious pleasure that comes of watching others open bags of new stuff is mind-bogglingly appealing to many, many people. No real statistics exist on how many of us have spent precious moments of our lives watching these strange, droning reveries, but there are an estimated one hundred thousand such videos released every week.[1] The first ten "YouTube haul" hits alone have a total of more than 180 million views.

And the appeal is not just about watching other people's "hauls." We privilege new stuff over used stuff, just as we prefer fats, meat, and carbs to plants, despite the fact that in study after study, plant-based diets have been proved to be healthier.[2] But, of course, meat, sugar, and carbs are yummy and, in the United States, cheap and plentiful besides. We need to work hard to eat "mostly plants." Like eating our vegetables, buying "mostly reclaimed" is something we must consciously prioritize. And, as with a healthy diet, we might come to realize that we actually prefer it in the long run.

CHAPTER 5:

Getting Good at Getting Used

Beware of all enterprises that require new clothes.
—Henry David Thoreau

This chapter is unique in that it's about things we *didn't* fix: it's about things we helped people to share. At our last pop-up, Good Stuff, we expanded our repair-shop model into a retail experience of healthy consumption. What that means in non-marketing jargon is that we rented a storefront in the Seaport District in downtown Manhattan and created a home on the ground level. We designed a dining room, a living room, a bedroom, closets, and, of course, included a repair shop in the back. We showcased "good new" stuff with the characteristics discussed in chapter 2—they were sustainably and ethically produced, well made, and repairable. We showcased "good used" stuff in a range of styles and prices. And we offered "good fixes," or repair services and workshops for all and sundry (people and objects), as in our previous shops. The purpose of this new pop-up was to depict what consumption might— or should—be like in the future. Our argument was that retailers and manufacturers looking to build a healthier, circular model will need to tap into a mix of good new, good used, and good fixes to create new revenue streams that support sustainable growth. And we wanted to show that for individuals, shifting to these new patterns is achievable, and even enjoyable.

One of the biggest mental and systemic shifts we wanted to explore was the rather ingrained idea that buying things almost by default means buying *new* things. In 2018, Americans spent some $4 trillion on new stuff, compared with $17.5 billion in used goods.[1] Despite the preponderance of new goods in our "stuff diets," perfectly good used things are all around us. Most important, used goods are becoming increasingly easy to obtain in reliable, "frictionless," and customer-pleasing ways that will be able to compete with the behemoth of Amazon, big-box retail, dollar stores, and the innumerable other fire hoses of consumption that shoot new stuff into your home with such astounding ease.

The Swap Haul and the Striped Top

During the second week of the pop-up, we held a clothing swap. We invited people to sign up online and to bring around five items of clothing to swap. The free event filled up days after we posted it, with a wait list dozens deep. On the day of, we set up our racks and watched women stream in, hungry to swap, and later emerge, satisfied.[2]

There was, as there always is, a fair amount of post-swap leftovers, unlucky items that didn't find a home in the frenzy of trading. I was excited, however, because these perfectly good remains represented, for me, an opportunity to go "shopping." Ever since my consumption crisis of conscience (sometime after I watched my hundredth or so load of scenery go into a dumpster), I have worn almost exclusively used clothing, except for shoes, underwear, and socks. I shop at thrift stores, or occasionally find second-hand garments online, but a swap represented an easy way for me to get some "new" clothes without even having to leave work. Ironically, for someone who works on consumption and who spent years working as a designer, I do not enjoy shopping and usually avoid or procrastinate until it's fairly dire. I'm also not a "vintage" fan in terms of my personal style; I don't wear obviously retro clothes, cat-eye glasses, or really anything particularly interesting. I like clothes that are easy to wear and functional (pockets!), that look good, that make me feel good, that will last a long time, and that are used.

For a reluctant and somewhat lazy shopper like me, the leavings of the swap were a gold mine. I picked up a wool blazer, a pair of maroon mid-calf-length pants, a pair of white cotton shorts, and a striped knit cowl-neck top. The wool blazer was a high-quality piece that I might have been reluctant or unable to buy new. All the items I found were successful "purchases," and went into fairly heavy rotation in my wardrobe, except for one. The striped shirt was a classic shopping mistake: the kind of garment that looks nice and that I think I will wear but, when I actually get it home, sits in my closet like an unwelcome toad. I pull it out periodically but somehow it never feels right, and it goes back into the closet to stare at me, unblinking, until I try (and fail) to wear it again.

Back when I used to buy new clothes, these types of shopping "mistakes" bothered me much more. First of all, new items are generally pricier than used ones, so a mistake feels like money flushed down the toilet. There is also guilt associated with buying something that you never wear; it feels wasteful to discard it. Numerous studies have shown that, despite the rise of a throwaway society, it still causes us "discomfort" to throw things away—especially things we deem to still have significant "utility" or belongings linked to our identity.[3] In one study, researchers gave subjects a cup of tap water and wrote the participants' names on the cups in Sharpie marker. Those whose names were written on the cup were 48 percent more likely to recycle their cups (as opposed to tossing them in the trash) than the people whose cups were unlabeled. Even for something as seemingly simple and "disposable" as a plastic cup, the authors of the study argue that "A decision to throw an identity-linked product in the trash symbolically represents an identity threat, as in essence you would be throwing a piece of your 'self' in the trash and by extension signaling to yourself that you must be worthless."

Disposing of those back-of-the-closet mistakes feels bad for at least three reasons—wasted money, lost utility, and, as revealed by the cup-recycling researchers, reduced self-worth. Lest you think we've gone off the rails here, raise your hand if you, too, have at least one "aspi-rational" (or "delusional") garment in the back of your closet that, in reality, you never, ever wear. These old mistakes and false conceptions of self lurking in the closet may indeed be part of our evolving identi-ties, so that never-worn jumpsuit may not only be a "mistake"; it may also feel like a missed opportunity, a hope or a fantasy never realized. Even Thoreau, certainly no fashionista, understood the role of clothing in our evolving identities:

> Perhaps we should never procure a new suit, however raggedy or dirty the old, until we have so conducted, so enterprised or sailed in some way, that we feel like new men in the old, and that to retain it would be like keeping new wine in old bottles. Our moulting season, like that of the fowls, must be a crisis in our lives.[4]

Figuring out what to wear is part of a continual process of molting and regrowth, and a few fits and starts are to be expected along the way.

Buying used doesn't necessarily reduce the number of these purchase fails; in my experience, that comes more with age and an increasingly honest awareness of what you actually look and feel good in. But buy-ing used means that the process of knowing and expressing yourself through clothes can be easier for you and much less harmful to others. That striped knit top will probably sit in my closet for another month or so, and then I will put it in the "pass it on" bag and send it back out to someone who will wear it. It came into my closet used, and will go into someone else's. I spent little (or in this case, nothing) on it in the first place. I shed those false feathers. I declutter my closet. And I keep a perfectly good item in circulation. When I buy used, the guilt—and therefore the stagnancy in my closet—of those failed purchases is lessened, as is the impact on my wallet and the planet.

The estimated emissions saved from buying a used shirt instead of a new one is 2.5 kg CO_2e (carbon dioxide equivalent), which amounts to the carbon absorbed by 127 trees in one day. So, not insignificant numbers, but still relatively small potatoes for one shirt. However, if you consider all the shirts purchased in America in one year, which is somewhere around 880 million garments, we are looking at a potential savings that exceeds 2.2 million tons of carbon annually in shirts alone.[5] The reason for this emissions savings is that, as we have seen, manufacturing and distributing new stuff takes a huge toll.

And there is plenty of used stuff to go around, at least for now. Thrift stores are flooded with donations—Goodwill stores in New York and New Jersey (one of 164 regional Goodwill areas) collected more than eighty-five million pounds of textiles in 2015. The United States is the leading exporter of used clothing worldwide, sending $700 million worth of used clothes overseas; in fact, over 60 percent of donated clothes in the States are exported. Finally, the EPA reports that more than fourteen million tons of clothing are incinerated or landfilled every year, while eight percent of out total landfill tonnage is clothing. Donating can often feel "green" or virtuous, but the fact of the matter is, donating alone is not enough. If we're not buying used ourselves, then we're just outsourcing the responsibility of "closing the loop," rather than accepting ownership of that responsibility along with ownership of our stuff.[6]

But if used stuff is so abundant, and if buying used is so fabulous— easing guilt, providing access to higher-quality goods, and reducing environmental impact—why do almost 50 percent of Americans report that they have not bought anything secondhand in the past year, and 60 percent say that they prefer buying new?[7] There are a number of barriers to buying used, both internal and external.

Intimate Apparel

In early 2008, before the birth of my first child, I had a "used only" baby shower. I had two older sisters with children, and several friends with small children, so it seemed logical to me to simply pass things along, and not buy a bunch of packaged, brand-new things. Most of the guests complied, though a few could not (or would not). Friends with children gave tiny clothes or blankets that were not too obviously soiled. Distant relations found the occasional used onesie or vintage set of blocks. From a few guests without children, the "no new stuff" edict elicited some creative gifts, such as a lovely mix CD of baby songs. A few people either did not have access to used goods or, more often the case, were puzzled by the theme of the party and simply did not want to give something secondhand.

My sisters, however, were thrilled to unload all their grotty old nursing bras, spit rags, gDiapers, breast pump paraphernalia, and various baby accoutrements—including an open pack of those enormous stretchy mom diapers they give you in the hospital for the first few days postpartum. Having shared clothes with my sisters my whole life (usually willingly, though perhaps sometimes without their knowledge in the teen years), I was thrilled with these less-than-pristine but eminently useful used gifts. While I was not at all grossed out, I distinctly remember a look of slight horror on the faces of a few of my guests as I held up a stretched-out belly band with frayed Velcro and a splotchy nursing pillow for them to ooh and aah over—so cuuute!

Many people understandably feel that used items are somehow

"contaminated" by the previous owners. One study interviewed respondents who "associate second-hand products with something dirty, disgusting, afflicting. Some of them believe that the clothes might remain with the prior owner's smell and/or essence." However, as with my sisters' stuff, "this barrier is diminished when participants know the seller of the product: the experience to get and to give something from/to family members and friends is very positive, pleasant, and common."[8] It is possible to reduce some of these internal barriers by changing our perception of value and our conception of contamination. Arguably, it's *new* things that are "contaminated," polluted by a toxic system that separates women working in garment factories from their children, pollutes rivers, and creates piles of cheap clothes that wind up getting incinerated. Once you have really seen the negative impacts of overproduction, the feeling that someone else's "essence" or micro-bugs or dander or whatever might be in my used sweater begins to seem surmountable, even taking into account understandable worries about infection or disease. Clothes can be washed, and objects can be disinfected. It's true that the closer to the body you get, the higher the barriers to buying used become; I have worn used (washed) undies that belonged to my sisters, but that's about it in the privates department. I'm not alone in this, as distance from the body seems to be a key factor in whether people will tolerate something used. While perhaps scientific evidence is not strictly necessary in this case, it's interesting to note that the aforementioned study authors confirmed that "some garments were more acceptable than others. People were more willing to wear shirts, sweaters, jackets or pants. What seemed to be completely intolerable though, were underwear, socks and bathing suits."

If you are willing to accept that buying used stuff has benefits, however, it may be worth finding ways to increase your capacity—to stretch that willingness to think about what can be found and used, used. Most people are open to to purchasing at least some things secondhand. My mother, perusing a draft of this book, commented that

> Wearing secondhand clothing is something I have never been able
> to enjoy. I have strong memories of revolting maternity clothes
> that were given to me because "you will never need those things
> later, so why buy?" or baby clothes for Lara given by Diane. I hated
> all that and it all disappeared as fast as I could find a garbage can
> or the Goodwill. . . . Now, furniture, dishes, glasses, silver, family
> stuff, as you know, I love all that.

Despite the lingering ick factor of those revolting clothes from half
a century ago, my mother delights in secondhand dishware. The key
is to start where you are—and then work your way up. By thinking
first about whether you can get something used, it's surprisingly easy
to significantly shift the percentage of used things you buy (or swap),
even without forcing yourself to share nursing bras with strangers. It's
an internal shift, a reassessment of "value," and an appreciation that old
and used might actually be better in many ways than new and toxic.
Simple awareness of the problem, and a commitment to start small and
begin with whatever "categories" of stuff seem manageable, can go a
long way to dismantling those internal barriers.

Clothing, Couches, and the Challenges of "Reverse Logistics"

Other barriers to buying used, however, are external, and removing them
might make it more likely that people will change their personal habits.
The main problems are logistical; it's often simpler, today, to purchase a
new sweater or chair or lamp than it is to purchase a used one. Online
or in stores, you can choose from seemingly infinite options organized
by style, color, price, brand. Vast amounts of human energy and ingenuity have been expended to make it astonishingly easy to make, market,

transport, and sell you almost anything in a matter of days. The term "frictionless" was coined to describe the ideal "user" (buyer) experience: never a hiccup or the hint of an obstacle to lessen the convenience for you, the customer, in opening your wallet.

In contrast, buying used is often still full of friction. Physical storefronts for new clothes vastly outnumber vintage shops. There are approximately twenty-five thousand thrift, resale, and consignment stores in the United States. (New York is home to just over 650 of them.)[9] In comparison, there are five times that number of shopping malls in the country—and that does not count individual storefronts.[10] For the consumer, it takes effort to find used goods, especially "good" used goods—though this challenge is actually getting easier, especially for clothing.

While new clothes are still prevalent, the resale market is growing twenty-one times faster than traditional retail. This resurgence of thrifting is in part a reaction to the rise of "fast fashion." The term, coined in 1989, refers to the accelerated pace that the clothing industry developed to churn out more garments and increase sales. Some retailers can push a fast-fashion garment from the design phase to your closet in as little as a week.[11] Fast fashion has grown remarkably over the past thirty years, and in 2018 represented a $35 billion market.[12] The staggering environmental impact of producing all this new clothing has been well publicized—as much as 1.2 billion tons of GHG emissions per year can be traced back to the apparel and textile industries, more than those of all international flights and maritime shipping combined.[13]

Partly as a backlash to this extreme situation, and partly because clothing reuse has a long and well-established history, the fashion industry is in many ways the most advanced in the "stuff" world in terms of tackling reuse. Reuse in clothing is catching up, especially online. Clothing rental services such as Rent the Runway, closet-sharing services like Gwynnie Bee, used-clothing online retailers like ThredUP, and peer-to-peer platforms like Poshmark, are only a few of the players in this exploding industry.[14] Despite these signs of change, it's still more frictionless and much more common to buy new.

In terms of non-clothing items, the landscape of reuse is even more imbalanced. I can order a new lamp—or ten thousand of them—online in the blink of an eye. Ordering a used lamp is more complicated. One of the main reasons for this disparity is the challenge of "reverse logistics." Very simply, for well over a century, we have been working to develop an incredibly powerful and efficient global system of production and distribution. But the system is designed to work only one way. I can order anything I want, let's say a lamp, from anywhere around the globe, and have it on my doorstep tomorrow. But if I am done with it, getting that lamp back out of my home and into the home of someone else is not easy. It's not really any more complicated than the system we currently have for delivery; it would just have to work in reverse: someone would have to pick it up, or I'd have to take it somewhere. It needs to be tracked, photographed, and therefore easily searchable. These are things we do incredibly well already. We just don't do them in reverse. Yet.

One of the first challenges to the "logistics of used" is storage—that is, inventory. Where do you keep the lamp or the knit top in the time between when the old owner decides they don't want it anymore and the new owner figures out where it is and purchases it? Second, how do you track the items and make them searchable and therefore findable? New objects are made in large batches, and are identical. When dealing with used merchandise, each item is unique. Finally, how do you get it out of the former owner's home and over to the new owner's address?

There are many exciting start-ups working in the area of used stuff, and a variety of ways they tackle these logistical challenges, depending on the items. There are two main models. One is to create a warehouse where the used items can be housed while they are on sale. For example, ThredUP, an online used clothing company founded in 2009, accepts items on consignment, photographs them, and keeps them in four giant warehouses in Pennsylvania, Illinois, Georgia, and Arizona. A centralized warehouse like this is possible for garments, since they do not take up a huge amount of space, can be folded and shipped for relatively low prices, and are not easily damaged in transport. But for breakable or bulky items (couches or lamps, for example), a centralized warehouse is impractical; it's expensive, and it increases the shipping costs and risk of damage. For years, Goodwill, Salvation Army, and other thrift stores allowed drop-off donations and maintained inventory in their stores. Increasingly, and especially in cities, this practice has become too costly.

The second model, pioneered by Craigslist and eBay, is a peer-to-peer system for used stuff. This means essentially using the homes or closets of the sellers as a distributed "warehouse," relying on the owners to photograph and enter details for whatever they want to sell, and requiring them to hold on to it until it is sold (or rented, in the case of peer-to-peer rental platforms). But the logistical challenge remains. How to get the couch from the first home to the second? The Craigslist solution of "figure it out yourself" or "find a man with a van" carries inherent limitations.

Other services are emerging to tackle this problem. AptDeco, one of our partners for Good Stuff, is a peer-to-peer marketplace for home furnishings and décor. If you have a couch or a lamp to sell (or buy), you can post it on AptDeco. The company keeps the site simple and easily searchable, it manages the transaction, and it provides delivery services. It's a bit like Craigslist but organized, limited to curated home furnishings, and much easier logistically. For the customer, the delivery option is critical; one of the inherent challenges of peer-to-peer is figuring out how to exchange the stuff without a ton of texts, awkward meetups, or failed handoff attempts. For the company, delivery is a big challenge—but a key to scaling reuse for non-clothing items. Managing pickups and deliveries is one of AptDeco's main innovations. It has developed proprietary software to help make that process as frictionless as it can be, and by doing so, it is able to maintain a much larger "warehouse" of searchable, curated items than it ever could in a central location. It's just got to make the search and transaction pleasant, and get the couch from me to you.

Centralized warehouses can still be a viable option, however. Another interesting company, called Yerdle, is tackling "reverse logistics" for manufacturer-retailers who would like to develop revenue streams from more than just selling new stuff. Unlike AptDeco, Yerdle is handling the "storage" issue with centralized warehousing. When I recently ordered a used camping cot from REI for my son Luke, the charge on my credit card statement appeared as "Yerdle." The cot had been purchased at REI and returned to the store, who then sent it to Yerdle. Yerdle repairs and refurbishes the cot, if needed, and posts it on REI's site, and then ships it to a happy eleven-year-old boy. This might seem like a lot of shipping, but the fact of the matter is that, even with all that transport, the environmental impacts of buying a used cot are much, much less than buying new. While it's better, of course, to buy local used goods if you can, even with shipping, used stuff is a better bet in terms of emissions. So, while the challenges of getting used stuff into a new owner's hands are still very real, diverse solutions are emerging from every corner of the market, and customers are catching on—or rather, being reminded of something really very ancient.

A Balanced Stuff Diet

In some ways, it is funny to watch us struggle to build a system of reverse logistics simply to re-create a practice that existed for millennia. Reusing and sharing clothing and home goods was once the norm. When textiles and furnishings required many hours of labor to make, they were passed down, handed over, remade, and repurposed until there wasn't anything left. Wills often listed "moveable property" like "Wearing Cloaths," tablecloths, napkins, pillowcases, and chests to keep them in. A brand-new item of clothing was once an achievement to make and a luxury to purchase. If this becomes the case again for new stuff, thanks to higher labor standards—and prices—start-ups and thrift stores and simple swaps like the one we hosted will become even more important in changing the ecosystem of shopping. And as for the occasional mistake, like my knit striped top, I will take it to my local thrift store or a used clothing drop-off point, or maybe I'll send it to ThredUP. I hope that someone else will find it, and wear it more often than I did. The other items I found at the swap will remain in heavy rotation for the foreseeable future.[15]

To those who might still have some reservations about buying used, I can only say that the shift in your stuff diet is worth it. Like resolving to eat your veggies, it can be hard to make the switch, and tempting to splurge too often. But if you start small and stick with it, your efforts will pay off. Clothing is often an appealing starting point for people beginning to rebalance their stuff diet (except, perhaps, for my mother), but the logic of "mostly reclaimed" applies to almost anything. Since Luke's "all used" baby shower eleven years ago, I slowly transitioned to an almost 100 percent reclaimed-clothes diet for the whole family. Furniture, housewares, and all kinds of other stuff followed naturally after. I spend less money on new stuff, which allows me a little margin to spend on alterations to make my clothes fit properly. (Clothes that fit well look much, much better—a good fit is more important than newness, take it from a costume designer.)

The slight additional effort required for this kind of sustainable consumption is a small price to pay, and it's easy to get better at buying secondhand very quickly. In my case, it's true that I had a fair bit of practice because of my long years of shopping for theatre designs, but there was still a learning curve. Over the years, I made a conscious attempt to rebalance my stuff diet: I now buy less overall, and when I do buy, I buy reclaimed as much as possible. As with most healthy dietary shifts, the long-term benefits outweigh the short-term effort. Best of all, as

PART IV

CARE FOR IT

Why should we bother to take care of our stuff? And what do we need to do it right?

We've established that we need stuff. We can identify good new stuff, and we know that we should buy mostly used stuff. Now that we have our good new or good reclaimed stuff, the next step is to care for it. For me, "care" includes repair, of course, as well as cleaning, putting things away, and general maintenance. Beyond these specific actions, care implies an overall sense of respect for the things we have: in the way we treat objects, acknowledge the resources and labor that went into them, and recognize their value in our lives.

One of the inescapable facts of repair, at least for now, is that it is unavoidably human. Perhaps in the future, bots such as Daisy or Liam or some other AI phenom will be able to perform all the various types of fixes we accomplished in our little shop. But at present, it is still relatively hard to systematize repair. The staggering volume and variety of objects out there make it hard to repeat tasks in an identical way. Even similar objects can break differently. (We fixed dozens of KitchenAid mixers, for example, each job a little bit different from the next.) It reminds me of theatre, where we create show after show, by hand, each one distinct from the previous one but also somehow the same.

Playwright Suzan-Lori Parks describes a pattern in her writing of "repetition and revision," a cyclical form of storytelling that for me captures this shared characteristic of theatre and repair.[1] Similar objects return to your workbench, wooden chair after wooden chair, the same but different, and your response to them is likewise both similar to the last time you worked on a chair but also changed: by what you learned the last time around, by the differences in the objects themselves, by how well you are working that day. Repair—as well as theatre—requires creativity, making unusual connections, and learning from disparate experiences. So, faced with an uncooperative glass butterfly, I might think of that weird glue that we used yesterday on a jewelry box, even though the two objects are completely unrelated. At the same time, there is a repetitiveness to repair; it's almost a formal dance, with creativity and expression bound by certain forms. Intake, diagnose, take it apart. Find parts, make it work, put it back together. Clean and shine, set the final price, and call the customer. Repeat and revise. In this simple dance, we can sometimes find, as Parks does in her writing, satisfaction, beauty, and even grace in the familiar things all around us.

CHAPTER 6:

Making and Mending in America

The greatness of America lies not in being more enlightened than any other nation, but rather in her ability to repair her faults.
—Alexis de Tocqueville

One chilly spring afternoon on the Upper West Side, Maria M. and her husband brought us a chipped plate painted with an image of the American novelist Zane Grey, along with a George and Mary cup, the lid to a little cat-shaped mug, and a ceremonial ivory spoon. This eclectic parade of slightly historical dinnerware got me thinking about the role of making and mending in American life. Historically, caring for our stuff was a necessary if somewhat unsung part of American culture. Making, mending's more celebrated older sibling, is at the heart of some of our most cherished origin stories. Today however, we make very little and mend even less. What have we lost in this transition?

The Zane Grey plate was off-white, with the portrait of the writer surrounded by a border of western landscapes. The plate was of a type mass-produced in the 1950s, a relic of the era's popular fascination with all things western, though Grey wrote primarily during the first decades of the century. *Riders of the Purple Sage*, one of Grey's best-known books, was published in 1912, though it takes place in 1872. Like most of Grey's ninety-plus novels, the book helped create and cement a twentieth-century conception of the nineteenth-century American West: vast landscapes with few rules, a place where self-sufficient men and spirited women built their own futures with their bare hands, and other staples of American myth. Stories like those presented by Grey lionized white settlers for "building" America, and largely ignored the role of Indigenous peoples and African Americans in shaping—making—this country. These stories, incomplete and distorted though they were, were repeated in words, on-screen, and on tchotchkes like the Zane Grey plate so often that they began to seem like historical fact. Though Grey's work was fiction, and often rather pulpy fiction at that, it mythologized themes that have long shaped the American story. But the plate—like the myth—was broken, and needed a little attention.

America, in Grey's stories and still to some extent in our collective myth, is a place where you can do anything, where you can be anything, where you can build your future yourself, whether you are making it with logs or with ones and zeros. It's home to the self-made man, whether he wears cowboy boots or hoodies. It's the land of linear progress, of straight highways running west, young man. It is, or was, a new country of unlimited resources and endless "progress": and it is our (when "our" refers mainly to white European males) manifest destiny to harness it and build our own futures in it.

Or so the story goes, anyway. The dream is looking increasingly threadbare in the twenty-first century, as resources prove to be manifestly *not* endless, and this history of expansion and exploitation of people and places continues to bear painful fruit. Nonetheless, the bildungsroman of the American West still influences many contemporary assumptions about what has value, what progress really means, and what kinds of labor matter.

The kind of labor that has value, according to some versions of the American myth, consists largely of two sorts: building something out of nothing (usually with unacknowledged and exploited labor) and then holding on to it against all comers, in a bid to "tame" or "civilize" the land and the people who originally lived on it. In *Riders of the Purple Sage*, Jane Withersteen, the fierce (but still in need of rescuing) Mormon heroine, has inherited a solid homestead in Utah, carved out of the "wild and purple wilderness" by her father, and "civilized" by Jane's feminine influence:

> In the massive blocks of stone and heavy timbers and solid doors and shutters showed the hand of a man who had builded against pillage and time; and in the flowers and mosses lining the stone-bedded stream, in the bright colors of rugs and blankets on the court floor, and the cozy corner with hammock and books, and the clean linened-table, showed the grace of a daughter who lived for happiness and the day at hand.[1]

The myth of literally *making* America, by hand, runs strong in our Western literature, from popular authors like Grey to the stories we read to children. Like Jane's father or Laura Ingalls Wilder's Pa, who could build a log cabin in a day or whittle a whatnot for Ma to place her cherished china shepherdess in, part of our national myth rests on the skill and capacity to carve homes out of the land to keep our families (and our stuff!) safe.

Stories like Grey's and Wilder's, though incomplete at best and racist and sexist at worst, did emerge in part from a fundamental truth: Americans of all kinds—Native, African, and European—were makers. From traditions of carving and woodwork (yes, log cabins, but also Haudenosaunee longhouses) to the rich traditions of African American quilting, we are indeed a nation built by people skilled at working with their hands.[2] This history became romanticized, and the contributions of nonwhites largely excised, in a process that tracks closely with the rise of industrialization.

This romanticization of American handcraft began earlier than Grey's novels or 1950s Westerns. In *The Age of Homespun*, historian Laurel Thatcher Ulrich describes a speech given by the minister and theologian Horace Bushnell in 1851. Bushnell extolled the humble colonial makers of American cloth, painting a picture of women spinning and weaving at home, the "queens of homespun" whose unlauded contributions were "the springs of our successes and the sources of our distinctions."[3] This vision of American homecraft was already a romanticized ideal; Bushnell gave his speech just as the era of factory-made textiles was taking off.

This pattern is familiar—repetition and revision. From Bushnell to Grey to our era, we have been enamored of the ideal of making: from homespun to the frontier to today's nostalgia for MADE IN THE USA. At least since Bushnell, the less Americans actually make, the more we romanticize making stuff. So perhaps it is no wonder that the little Zane Grey plate was made in the 1950s, canonizing our myths in a decade that arguably marked the final nail in the coffin of American homecraft and the beginning of the decline of American manufacturing.

We don't make a lot of stuff anymore, either at home or in factories—and we fix even less. From 1910 until the 1950s, about 32 percent of Americans worked manufacturing jobs; by 2015, only 8.7 percent did so.[4] In 1970, manufacturing represented 24.3 percent of GDP, double what it was in 2018.[5] Making in factories was linked to making at home. In the late 1990s sociologist Ruth Milkman found that many line workers at a (now closed) General Motors plant in Linden, New Jersey, did skilled handwork at home in their off-hours.[6]

Historian Susan Strasser has described nineteenth-century women's skill at handcraft, from hooked rugs to clothing to reupholstering chairs. Americans used to make a significant proportion of their clothing, tools, even furniture. And the (still) relatively high price of store-bought goods made it worth their while, well into the twentieth century. But as manufactured goods have gotten more plentiful and cheaper, and are increasingly made overseas, as women have entered the not-at-home workforce, and as our population has grown more urban and more professional, skilled handcraft of all kinds has declined.

Many of our customers expressed a lack of confidence in working with their hands, like Maria with the Zane Grey plate. It was just a simple chip, it seemed like a lot of effort to bring it to us, and we wondered why she didn't just fix it herself at home with a dab of Krazy Glue. She explained to us, as did many other customers, that she just didn't feel as though she'd do a good job at it. Many of the botched DIY jobs we re-repaired in our shops seem to indicate that Maria was not alone in her lack of skills. We scraped a lot of old glue off the work of valiant but perhaps overenthusiastic ceramic fixers, not to mention the numerous chair leg joints we encountered that were poorly, sometimes violently repaired at home—expanding foam glue sprayed hopefully at the outside of a joint, screws brutally driven through the spindles at incoherent angles—it's enough to make you grateful for Maria's prudence in just bringing the poor plate to us. On the brighter side, many of our handier customers shared their skills and tips with us, or expressed nostalgia for a time when they, or their parents, made and fixed their own stuff. A few of them were even inspired to take up the task themselves, reporting back that after we had completed a job for them, they decided to tackle their own lamp or chair. In general, though, the picture both in our shops and more broadly is one of a steady decrease in confidence and skill in working with our hands. Strasser draws a direct line from this decline in making and mending to our transformation into a consumer society or, as she more bluntly puts it, to becoming "trashmakers."

Despite this rather depressing transformation from makers to trashmakers, the urge to create is still with us—witness the rise of the maker movement over the past decades, the proliferation of craft shops on Etsy, and the glut of home-makeover shows. I include cooking programs in this category; cooking is a form of making that is still very prevalent, and enormously popular in our media. Surfing between *Flip or Flop* on HGTV, *The Great British Baking Show* on Netflix, and a dozen other reality shows, it is possible to spend an entire twenty-four-hour period watching other people make things. And while these programs don't actually count as making for the viewer, they certainly scratch what is apparently a very big itch in our society; if we don't build anything anymore, at least we can watch someone else do it.

The Price of Not Making

Alex Langlands is a British archaeologist whose work both scratches the watch-other-people-make-stuff itch *and* explores the deeper need behind our love of shows about redecorated family rooms and towers constructed of meringue. Langlands was a host of a series of British reality TV shows, including *Going Medieval, Edwardian Farm, Victorian Farm*—you get the idea. These shows, much like a visit to an old-timey reconstructed village, allow the viewer to imagine inhabiting the world in a way that is no longer accessible, but still deeply resonant for many people. Apparently, Langlands's years of wearing tweed and sowing potatoes while pretending to ignore modern-day film crews helped him to develop a comprehensive understanding of the appeal—and power—of making. (Presumably, his training as a historian helped too.) His book *Cræft* chronicles Langlands's years of toiling on everything from traditional medieval fences to bee skeps, using seriously rustic materials and methods. Knee deep in cow patties and river reeds, Langlands argues, with the unassailable credibility of a person who has actually *done it*, that in the making of things lies a combination of physical skill, knowledge, power, and resourcefulness, which he calls "cræft."

The word comes from Old English, and Langlands takes care to point out the difference from our modern conception of craft, or simply the ability to make things with our hands. His argument is that cræft is a way of thinking and interacting with the world that is fundamental to our species, and that is now in danger of being lost: "Against a rising tide of automation and increasing digital complexity, we are becoming further divorced from the very thing that defines us: we are makers, crafters of things." Or we once were.

People have been worried about losing our identity as makers for a long time. Ralph Waldo Emerson, who was born more than two hundred years ago, and one hundred years before the Edwardian era Langlands so cheerfully re-created on TV, was already well aware of what we lose when we give up our ability to make. He imagines a cræfty fellow who makes all his belongings, and then passes the stuff on to his son. The knowledge and power stay with the maker, and are lost to the poor kid, who simply becomes the inheritor, or what today we might call a consumer: "The advantages of riches remain with him who procured them, not with his heir. . . . Not only health, but education, is in the work." The hapless non-making second generation is left with a pile of "commodities" (Emerson-speak for "stuff"), but without all the nice educational benefits that come from putting his labor into making them. Worse, having now got all the stuff, he is basically enslaved by it all:

When he comes to give all the goods he has year after year collected, in one estate to his son . . . and cannot give him the skill and experience which made or collected these . . . the son finds his hands full, not to the use of these things, but to look after them and defend them from their natural enemies. . . . We have now a puny, protected, person guarded by walls and curtains, stoves and down beds, coaches . . . and who, bred to depend on all these, is made anxious by all that endangers those possessions, and is forced to spend so much time in guarding them, that he has quite lost sight of their original use, namely, to help him to his ends, to the prosecution of his love, to the helping of his friend . . . and he is now what is called a rich man—the menial and runner of his riches.[7]

A century before the rise of the consumer republic, Emerson identifies a populace that is hampered rather than supported by its stuff, and was brought to this state by the loss of manual connection, of making.

In today's version of this Emersonian conundrum, we don't necessarily inherit our stuff, but we are nonetheless divorced from making it because we have freed ourselves, manually, mechanically, technologically, and economically, from crafting any of our own "hardware, wooden-ware, carpets, cloths, provisions" and just about anything else. And we too face Emerson's harsh sentence—the subject-object relationship becomes reversed and we become burdened, a servant to our stuff. This burden— this over-entanglement—is compounded because in being divorced from making it, we have also lost the "skill and experience" to fix it.

Making and Fixing

In the mid-1980s, Douglas Harper's car broke down. Harper was a sociologist who had moved to northern New York State to teach, and he drove a Saab station wagon. When the car needed work, Harper was directed to a nearby auto-repair shop owned and operated by Willie, a local fixture and semi-legend. Willie fixed Harper's car, just as he took care of almost all the locals' vehicles. But Harper stuck around, fascinated by the culture of Willie's shop, and curious about the man and the skills behind the repairs. Harper turned his observations into *Working Knowledge*, a book that is simultaneously a detailed portrait of the artist as an older repairman and an outsider's guide to decoding the work of the skilled fixer.

Harper's study of Willie is a somewhat reverent and occasionally bemused record of a dying breed. Willie is among the last of his type; he is an independent, somewhat ornery tinker-toolmaker whose social role Harper traces back all the way to the Iron Age. Harper places Willie in a lineage of not just fixers but also makers and fabricators and craftspeople of all kinds. (Happily, these strange birds still survive today in large numbers in the backstage world of theatre, and in our repair shops, as we will see in the next chapter.) According to Harper, creation and repair are really one category of action: "Fixing and making are but different points along a continuum." Both practices require a sensitivity to the object itself: an understanding of the tasks it is supposed to perform and familiarity with the component materials. Making requires a prospective understanding of the tasks that will be required to be performed, while fixing requires a retrospective look at what used to occur. Both require creativity and patience.

Harper is right: it's relatively easy to fix things if you know how to make them in the first place. It's why, in our shops, we hired theatre people like ourselves, people used to making all kinds of stuff. Emerson wrote that "a man who supplies his own want, who builds a raft or a boat to go a-fishing, finds it easy to calk it, or put in a thole-pin, or mend the rudder." For those who don't know what a thole-pin is, Strasser put it even more simply a hundred years later in *Waste and Want*: "Repair ideas come more easily to people who make things. If you know how to knit or do carpentry, you also know how to mend a torn sweater or repair a broken chair. . . . Indeed, mending and restoring objects often requires even more creativity than original production."[8]

Strasser describes, for example, how women who were capable of making a dress from scratch, but who did not always have the means, would use repair techniques to do what we would call "upcycling," and they called "making over": "The term covered a lot of territory: simple hemming, dyeing or treating worn fabrics, covering frayed cuffs and collar with handmade needlework or machine made braiding, or completely disassembling a garment and using the pieces for some other purpose." Proficiency in making naturally supported repair and frugality, and connected households to a nineteenth-century circular economy. When a garment could no longer be repaired or made over for children, it would be turned into rags and used for rugs or other household purposes. When finally even the rags were done, they were bought by the itinerant "rag man" and turned into paper. In other words, women who knew how to make clothing were able to increase the life span of their clothes by mending and remaking a multitude of garments and, in so doing, to fuel a larger production process. The challenge for us today is to take these frayed but still extant threads of myth, and making, and mending in our culture, and weave them in to our modern lives: it's no small task.

A Big Load for One Little Plate

Maria's chipped Zane Grey souvenir links us to an inherited notion of the role of making in American myth. Tied up in our creation stories is the perception that Europeans "built" this country, from raw earth, an idea that leaves a lot out—most important, the presence of Indigenous peoples whose populations numbered in the millions, who already inhabited this land before Europeans began homesteading here, and who practiced their own traditions of making and of maintenance; likewise overlooked is the forced labor of millions of African Americans whose contributions are often not accurately represented in our American myth. Beneath this often romanticized and incomplete mythology, there does lie the truth that the vast majority of our ancestors in this country—all of them, Indigenous, African, European, and others from all over the globe—possessed the capacity to make, and therefore to care for, stuff. This historical capacity to make spanned social classes and is the often-unrecognized reality underlying our mythology of nation building, of progress, of what it means to be American.

We prioritize and romanticize our history of making: our American concept of progress is tied to the creation of new stuff—gadgets, homes, shopping centers, cities. Yet we have moved away from the reality of making and have become more likely to embrace reality TV *about* making. So while we still romanticize making—from our myth of the West to our home-makeover-show binges—many of us have lost the opportunity, and the ability, to actually make anything ourselves. So, we are left with the myth, the fetish of the new, but without the deep, kinesthetic knowledge of the things around us. Disconnected from making, we are even more distanced from the next point on the continuum, mending. We have neglected our long and partially forgotten tradition of care and stewardship. And finally, in this distance from making and mending, we have lost a form of communication, one of our major modes of expression as human beings. We have ceded that creative power of thought and communication to impersonal systems larger than ourselves, over which we have little control.

So how do we regain control or, better yet, balance? The answer is not a knee-jerk nostalgia for the past, neither for the days of homecraft nor for the more modern, Trumpian fantasy of a return to large-scale manufacturing in the United States. Those days are gone, socially, economically, and hopefully, environmentally. But perhaps there is a future where the primacy of making in our society—the myth of progress, of building a new world around us—is balanced by a higher value on maintenance, on stewardship, on repair. And one simple way toward that balance is to care for what we have, gluing the chipped plate together and slowly, piece by piece, rebuilding—repairing—our myths (and the plates that carry them).

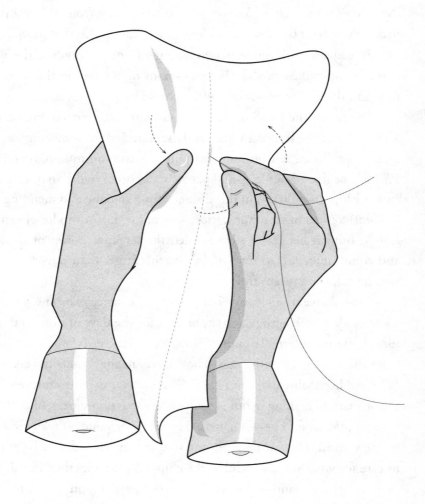

CHAPTER 7

The Fixers

I hear and I forget. I see and I remember. I do and I understand.
—often recycled and usually (mis)attributed to Confucius

During the years I was running our repair shops, I also continued to design scenery and costumes for theatre. I moved back and forth between the world of make-believe and the real world, and wherever I turned, I was dealing with stuff. In theatre, choosing it, drawing it, buying it, building it, painting it. In the repair shops, cleaning it, opening it, fixing it. (And in both worlds, constantly schlepping it around.) Toggling between worlds, I was able to compare these two supposedly distinct realms of fact and fiction and learn the ways in which they are similar. It turns out that there are a few things those of us who supposedly live in the real world all the time might learn from the people who make the make-believe: People who make and fix—who have *craft*. People like those I have worked with all my life, in the theatre. People who are skilled at a certain kind of problem-solving that is very common, it turns out, both backstage and in repair shops: creative, ingenious, on-budget, and on-time handcraft for all sorts of stuff. People whose skills are becoming rare, or niche, or devalued, but whose way of working has something valuable to teach all of us.

Many of the fixers in our repair shops over the years came from the backstage worlds of theatre, TV, and film (as did I). This is because, in the course of creating worlds onstage, theatre people learn how to make things and how to fix all sorts of things. We may hot-glue plastic food to walls one day and install neon tubing the next. I have worked with wood, fabric, steel, aluminum, plastic, sand, earth, garbage, plants both fake and real. (Let's not talk about the small graveyard plot we covered with real sod and had to take outside every night after the show so it could get some sun the next day!) We make things from scratch, like the beautiful miniature dollhouses a team of assistants and students built for one show, as many as five people stuffed in my small studio, crouched over the basswood houses on makeshift work surfaces. We buy new and we hunt for antiques. We adapt and modify. We create Frankensteins; I recall, if not fondly then at least with bemusement, the twin stuffed plush monkeys we created for a musical, wired to forever pose on branches—one brown and naturalistic, one "dipped" in gold, branch and all. Imposing steel structures or diminutive gold plushies, it's all in a day's work.

We think about how objects are built, how they will look to others, how they will perform, how long they need to last, how much they should cost, what they should look like, and, of course, what kind of worlds they will help create. For we realize, in theatre, that creating worlds is a two-way street. Every object onstage needs to fit the rules of the world that we make up, and in turn, every object we put in it helps define that world.

A play is like a little universe, or like the inside of a sort of messy clock. To make sure the machinery moves properly, everything has to play its part reliably, from the actors to the crew, from the moving scenery down to the humblest prop. An object that makes it onstage has a very particular job to perform. Finding the perfect prop for the job can be an exhaustive process. Every prop is carefully researched, then found or made, then vetted by designers, directors, actors. Every item gets its tryout in rehearsal, tested for look, for compatibility with the actor and scene, for safety and durability. Every item is tracked in detailed paper-work called prop lists and run sheets. And backstage during the show, every item has its place—even the smallest prop has a home, outlined in tape and carefully labeled, on the prop table. This attention to detail—this care—goes for every prop, every show, every time. (Of course, we also torture, misplace, and misuse objects as well; the order of the prop table on opening night is usually equal and opposite to the chaos in the shop or the prop storage area. Theatre has externalities too.)

And so, for the short time that the artificial world of a production exists, every prop has a role to play in keeping the clockwork moving, in telling the story. Each object, no matter how silly or mundane, matters. In real life, however, we sometimes don't notice how the things we bring into our homes and build into our lives—our props—contribute to our own stories. At home, we are moving and speaking on a little set of our own making . . . and perhaps we might do well to learn a bit about how to see the small things around us as a vital part of the meaning we create each day. One way to get there is to see the world, at least for a moment, through the eyes and hands of the people who work on our props, and our broken stuff.

Who Are the Fixers in Your Neighborhood?

In our shops the three main fixers were my husband, Michael, our col-league Adam, and me. Each of us had a few special areas in which we were particularly confident; Michael specialized in carpentry, lamps, and oddball projects, Adam did all appliances and electronics, and I cov-ered jewelry, paint, and ceramics. We also had a rotating cast of fixing characters that included Flora, Simo, Kim, Laura, Mike D., Chris, India, Stephanie, Maria, Chimmy, and many more. Most of these fixers had, like us, certain types of materials or objects they felt especially comfortable with. A few fell into the true genius category, people so skilled with their hands (and minds!) that they could tackle virtually anything.

My husband, Michael, is one such person: while he may be most comfortable with carpentry, he really can fix anything. (He asked me not to write that but I'm doing it anyway because it really is true.) He can figure out any physical object, from a broken pen to automated moving scenery on Broadway. He can tie all kinds of knots and unscrew jars and generally make objects behave the way they are supposed to. He is the kind of person you would want with you on a desert island not only because he's easy to get along with but because he could crack coconuts, or rig up a shelter, or fashion an SOS transmitter before you could say "MacGyver."

Our other star fixer was Adam, an eccentric and shy teddy bear sort of guy who makes beautiful lamps and clocks from found objects he has collected over the years from all over the country. Adam has been tinkering, making, and fixing since he was a child, and he claims that his current facility with things and how they work is grounded in the time he spent taking things apart as a kid. His understanding of stuff is astounding and agnostic; he is comfortable fine-tuning solar-powered systems for an outdoor art installation but also perfectly happy cleaning gunk out of a blender. Like many artists and makers, waste bothers Adam. He spent time after Hurricane Katrina picking up trash left out on the streets of New Orleans. Some of the materials he collected still look like debris, and some have been transmogrified into elegant digital clocks or LED lamps. In various states of transformation, these reclaimed items populate his workspace, which he has quietly and steadily transformed from a grungy auto body shop in Brooklyn into a beautiful art-and-tinker shared workspace, which he and his partner, Julie, dubbed

Workshopopolis. This fertile workshop was the site of much of our fixing over the six years since our first pop-up, where Adam's area of expertise was electronics, appliances, audio equipment, toasters, fans, sewing machines—basically everything that plugs in, beeps, whirs, spins, or lights up.

In addition to Michael and Adam, I myself did a lot of the fixing work in the shop. I am nowhere near as skilled as either of them, but I did have a lot of experience making things for theatre, specifically small-scale set models, painting scenery, and sewing costumes or the occasional curtain or drop for the stage. This experience translated fairly well to the shop, where my comfort with tiny tiny things (a chair made for a 1:48 set model—where a quarter inch represents one foot—is about the size of a lima bean, and I have made hundreds of these types of things over the years), plus a willingness to just try anything, made me the resident expert for jewelry, ceramics, most jobs involving paper, some stitching, and paint treatments, stains, or touch-ups. Sometimes the work was boring, like tying a million tiny knots between each bead on a necklace. Sometimes it was quite fun, like rebuilding an entire missing piece from a clay sculpture, which I did using paper towel and white glue and which came out looking surprisingly great. Often it was satisfying, like touching up a small stool painted with a tiger, for a little kid.

As for the many others who joined us in the shop, their skills and their backgrounds varied. Flora, like Michael and Adam, is somewhat of a natural stuff genius. Though she didn't have as many years of experience, she had an uncanny ability to just figure things out. I was floored when she cracked a stuck suitcase combination lock simply by turning the dials, listening, and feeling the slight clicks of the tumblers until she hit upon the correct combination, and when she taught herself to handweave the cane seat on a chair. All the fixers, experts and novices alike, learned and improved by doing, with help from one another. What everyone had in common was some ability to work with their hands to solve problems. I should be more specific—we all not only worked with our hands but *thought* with them too.

Repair in Body and Mind

I once watched Michael help our then ten-year-old son with a fun little paper-folding challenge Luke had brought home from school. The assignment involved folding Post-it notes into different shapes: triangles with half the area of the original Post-it, squares with one-quarter of the area, and so on. The challenges got increasingly difficult until Luke was stumped by the last Post-it brain-bender. Michael started fiddling with the Post-it, and as I watched his hands turn the paper over, I knew he would get it. I knew because I've observed that same interplay between mind and hands in him before, as he turns over a broken screen or wiggles a piece of scenery that is not behaving. I can *see* him literally thinking with his hands and I know that he'll be able to crack it with a combination of intellectual and manual knowledge. As Douglas Harper observed in his study of Willie's auto shop, Michael's hands are not incidental to the problem-solving; they are part of the thought process.

It's that ability to decode through the interplay of mind and hand—that kinesthetic knowledge—that makes Michael so invaluable in the repair shop. While there is a fair bit of repetition in repair (over the years, we tackled more than 200 wobbly chairs, 400 broken lamps, and 150 broken ceramics), there is also a specificity to each problem, just as there is both repetition and revision in theatre. Each show is slightly different, but we have a process that works for all of them. Similarly, each of those 200 wobbly chairs might have been built in exactly the same way, but they might break in 199 different ways. And so, you need a process for approaching each broken object—and each customer. In our shop, we called this initial step in the repair process the "diagnosis."

People often sent us photos of broken objects, and while that's somewhat helpful, it's much harder for Michael to diagnose when he can't touch the item. When a wobbly chair is right there, for example, Michael can pick it up, torque it a bit, and look at the joints. It's usually enough for him to know whether it needs to be broken down and reglued completely, or if it is what we called a "simple de-wobble," where you can inject glue into the joints, clamp it, and tighten the whole structure without completely taking it apart. Sometimes it seems like magic. How can he know from just picking up a chair whether it is a twenty-minute fix or a three-hour job? Some might call it intuition. This was an important point for us in our repair shops, because if it's just intuition, that means it can't be taught or easily replicated.

We're not the first fixers to worry about this question. Harper observed this pattern as well, and points out that "intuition is a word often used for something we don't understand." He decodes intuition at Willie's repair shop, breaking it down into a "kinesthetic sense" married with a knowledge of materials and a dose of "rationalized" or "by-the-book" learning. What seems like intuition or magic is really a subtle interplay among acquired knowledge, rational assessment of the problem, physical knowledge of materials, and physical sensitivity to the specific object. Combined, these form the foundation of what Harper called kinesthetic or working knowledge and Langlands called cræft: an ability to think with hands and mind together that indeed adds up to a special form of wisdom.

As a creature of the theatre and as an anchor in the repair shop, Michael has worked with everything from sand to steel, but his true love is carpentry. He knows how different kinds of trees grow, how their wood breaks, how it reacts to being cut or sanded. He has acquired "rational" knowledge by reading books and talking with other experts (as I write this, he is devouring a page-turner called *Understanding Wood*), and he also has the embodied knowledge of simply working with the materials for years. So, Michael is able to pick up a chair (or a Post-it) and arrive at a solution informed by hand and mind.

It turns out it's not just Michael or other repair wizards who have this capacity. This quality of thinking with both body and mind is something that many people have. In fact, all people have it. Learning, memory, and our ability to communicate—indeed, our ability to think—are based on an interplay between mind and body that is central to all human beings, not just repair wizards. In *How the Body Knows Its Mind*, cognitive scientist Sian Beilock gives dozens of examples of how thinking is improved when it is connected with the body. Third graders are given sentences to read, like "Pete gives each hippo seven fish," "Then he gives each alligator four fish." Students who are allowed to act out the sentences with little toy hippos and fish are more likely to solve associated math problems than students who simply read the story. Students grasp difficult math concepts by exploring them with a "math dance." Dancers learn choreography by practicing the motions. Actors memorize lines by associating them with their blocking. Test subjects solve a complicated puzzle by being encouraged to move their body in a way that mimics the solution. Children who play the piano have better math skills. In short, "your body helps you learn, understand, and make sense of the world."[1] This concept of "embodied cognition" helps identify and parse the seeming magic or intuition that we use in our repair shops to diagnose and fix. It's not magic or intuition; it's simply an additional dimension of thought and knowledge that we often overlook or "misunderestimate" because our society currently privileges only a few forms of knowledge—and power. In naming and recognizing this powerful form of cognition, we can begin to value it again, and understand how to teach it.

Teaching Intuition

Like Michael, Adam has the ability to pair rationalized knowledge (book learning) with working knowledge (embodied cognition). His capacity to think with body and mind served him well in the shop, especially for the trickiest part: diagnosis. To figure out what is wrong with something, Adam will pick up an object to feel how it moves, he'll listen to it, and of course he'll open it up and look at it. He even smells it—he will sometimes detect a smoky odor that lets him know a motor has burned out. He uses all his senses *and* his extensive rationalized knowledge of how these objects are made and how they work. The question for us in the shop, as we grew and needed more fixers, was, did we need to *find* more Adams and Michaels, or could we train them? How could we replicate a genius, especially when our current educational systems seem to privilege only one part of the knowledge equation?

For increasingly, we have learned to ignore or devalue kinesthetic knowledge, as well as forgotten how to teach it. As Beilock observes,

> Probably more than any other institutions, Western mainstream education embraces the computer metaphor of the mind. Even though the information we take in comes from five different senses—visual, aural, smell, taste, and touch—educators tend to characterize the storage of this information as abstract, removed from the very senses that helped load the mind's hard drive in the first place. . . . This stationary model of education is counterproductive, because we tend to learn through movement and engaging with people and things in our environment.[2]

This type of lopsided approach is a disadvantage not only to the child trying to add hippos and fish or the repair shop owner trying to find new fixers but to society at large. Langlands argues that overprivileging a "formal knowledge approach leads to an inability to entertain alternative ways of thinking and doing—or alternative forms of knowledge." Over centuries, we have moved away from models of learning that might involve the body, and have elevated rationalized knowledge to the point where it is often perceived as the only form of knowledge. Large numbers of people used to learn, for example, in a master-apprentice setting, where rationalized knowledge could be passed on while, at the same time, giving the student the chance to practice needed skills, or in other words, to embody the knowledge.

Perhaps because repair requires both these types of knowledge, the master-apprentice model seems to be a common component in the origin stories of our repair geniuses (and a fair number of other geniuses, too, as it turns out). Almost every maker or tinkerer I have met or read about seems to have a charming tale of an uncle or grandfather or aunt who helped them to develop their craft. From Willie in the auto shop, who learned to work a forge at age seven, to Steve Jobs, whose dad taught him how to take things apart and put them back together, to Adam dissecting a Bose radio, each genius has had the opportunity to learn by doing, often alongside an expert.[3]

With dozens of fixers of varying degrees of skill and experience in our shop, we saw over and over how important it was to simply be able to work side by side in order to learn. More skilled fixers caught on quickly, but still benefited from being able to ask questions and receive pointers quickly. Eager but not necessarily skilled volunteers often needed the opportunity to learn the ropes and practice the techniques with an experienced fixer near enough so mistakes could be spotted and disasters averted, but with enough independence to try to struggle through on their own.

The master-apprentice model is an ancient form of passing on both rationalized knowledge and physical skills. But what does that mean for the future of repair as a robust sector of a thriving, sustainable, circular economy? How do you create more Michaels, Adams, and Floras? How do you build a system where they can earn a living wage with their kinesthetic genius? How do you teach hundreds or thousands of people in a master-apprentice format? How do you scale something that is inherently local, often artisanal, and so intimately tied to a way of working rooted in the past?

Scaling Repair

There are lots of factors in scaling repair; legal issues such as intellectual property, access to manuals and parts, economic incentive structures and international labor patterns that make it hard to compete, and the challenges of reverse logistics. This is a critical piece of the puzzle—we need legislation like that being championed by the Right to Repair movement, which will compel manufacturers to make their products fixable at independent shops and by consumers, not just by licensed dealers. We need international labor laws that ensure fair pay to people making stuff around the world, so that prices for new goods simply can't be artificially cheap anymore. And, unless we start making robots for repair, which seems unlikely at this point given the variability of the tasks, we'll need to train a workforce if we want to expand our capacity to fix things, and to bring repair and service into a circular, sustainable economy. This will involve creating systems where people can again learn, in body and mind, the necessary skills. It will also involve recalibrating (or repairing, if you will) our concept of *how* to scale, and what innovation looks like.

Since mending and making are so closely linked, repair fans might look to the maker movement for some ideas on how to grow. The term "maker movement"[4] was coined in the early years of this century, and described a trend that united tech enthusiasts, artisans, and hackers who attempted to revive and modernize the tradition of individual making and tinkering. Like repair, the maker movement was characterized by diverse, artisanal, and decentralized work—and therefore faced challenges to scaling. Chris Anderson, CEO of 3D Robotics and former editor in chief of *Wired,* grappled with this question in his 2012 book,

Makers: The New Industrial Revolution. Anderson proposed a new form of scaling that is "both small *and* global. Both artisanal and innovative. Both high-tech and low-cost. Starting small but getting big. And, most of all, creating the sort of products that the world wants but doesn't know it yet, because those products don't fit neatly into the mass economies of the old model. The money on the table is like krill: a billion little entrepreneurial opportunities that can be discovered and exploited by smart creative people."[5]

Anderson's vision for an artisanal movement connected by the power of modern technology provides a template for repair, as well. The ability to crowdsource wisdom, in the form of YouTube videos or iFixit guides, can make a repair rabbit hole avoidable, or at least salvageable. The growing community of fixers, connected by such groups as Repair.org, Repair Cafés, and iFixit, allows people to share ideas, hone business models, and push for legislative and corporate policies that support stewardship over waste. And open-source knowledge and platforms can allow fixers to be local, while tapping into resources beyond their own community.

One important mind-set shift is to realize that inherent challenges (smallness, master-apprentice model, individualized work) are not actually liabilities to scaling repair, but might be the solution: the seeds for a powerful new-old model. Our current economy fetishizes the new, the shiny, the high-tech miracle, and devalues anything that is not seen as "innovative." In a *New York Times* op-ed titled "End the Innovation Obsession," David Sax challenges our very definition of innovation, and provides an antidote to the endless push for the silver bullet:

This mind-set equates innovation exclusively with invention and implies that if you just buy the new thing, voilà! You have innovated! Rearview innovations have proved to be as transformative as novel technologies. . . . They are innovative precisely because they propose a valuable community alternative solution. This type of reflective innovation requires courage, because it calls into question the assumption that newer is necessarily better. These innovations aren't mired in the past. They are solutions firmly focused on the future—not some technocentric version of it, where we invent our way to utopia, but a human-centric future that reflects where we've been, what we've learned and how we actually want to live.[6]

The key, however, is in the mix of old and new. You can't forget the "rearview" part of rearview innovations. The internet can support and enhance master-apprentice learning, but it's hard to beat being in the same room with someone you are learning from. Platforms like Handy.com or TaskRabbit can facilitate connections between fixers and customers, but there is nothing like actually knowing and trusting the people who work on your stuff. Scaling repair will need to be a hybrid: open sourced, digitally interconnected, supported by technology and policy, but also local, individual, and deeply connected to person, place, body, and hand. The type of creative problem-solvers who fuel the nascent repair movement, as well as their kindred spirits in theatres, artists' studios, maker labs, and home workshops around the country, are the front lines as we rearview-revolutionize the way we make and mend, and what we value.

CHAPTER 8:

God and Stuff

Objets inanimés avez-vous donc une âme
Qui s'attache à notre âme et la force d'aimer?

Inanimate objects, do you have a soul
which cleaves to our soul and forces it to love?
—Alphonse de Lamartine

You know by now that we fixed a lot of quotidian objects over the years: we slogged through piles of fans and forks, dug gunk out of hundreds of plastic pearls, and generally scrubbed and straightened and shined a heck of a lot of . . . Shinola. But before you judge us as hopelessly tethered to "treasures on earth, where moth and rust destroy,"[1] you might be heartened to know that we occasionally looked up from the moth and rust and glimpsed something larger.

While many discussions of spirituality, from Buddhism to the Bible, point to a rejection or at least a deep suspicion of material things, all our de-wobbling and de-gunking somehow made me wonder if God can, in fact, be in the details. Of all the humble and inarguably earthbound objects we fixed, a few objects dared speak to a higher order, elevating our work ever so slightly and providing us a connection with some of the higher—or deeper—forces that shape the way we treat our stuff, and maybe even the way we treat our planet.

A wooden sign, a collection of seven Bhagavad Gitas, and a chi revitalizer open an exploration of how spirituality, religion, myth, and the social and legal codes they underlie shape the way we think about ownership and stewardship. Do Judeo-Christian creation beliefs steer many of us toward a mentality of exploitation and waste? Does Hinduism offer an alternative emphasis on not only creation but also maintenance? And how might maintaining our chi—or at least our chi revitalizers—speak to a larger shift in values?

God's Gifts

In the early summer of 2017, a broken wooden sign was delivered unto us in Inwood. The plaque was about five feet long and five inches high, with routed edges, shaped ends, and an enlarged center section. The brass letters were falling off so that the sign was in imminent danger of no longer reading DEUS NOBIS HAEC OTIA FECIT. This phrase from Virgil is the motto of the city of Liverpool and is variously translated as "God has given us this ease" or "God has made these comforts for us." Amid the sometimes drudgery of schlepping and fixing all these things and my more-than-occasional complaints about how much work or how little time I had, the wooden sign stopped me in my tracks. I read it as a reminder that we have been blessed with so much here in the United States, and that *I* have been blessed with so much, that I'd better not forget to appreciate all that we have in this world. The message of the sign seemed to be: "You've been given a lot, so be thankful, dammit."

The sign and my reading of it contain two major assumptions, or beliefs. The first is that God made the world and everything in it.

The second is that he (or she or they) made it *for us*. This idea does not only appear on decorative plaques in Inwood. In fact, it is central to Judeo-Christian theology and underlies the way that many of us (including me, until I started researching it a bit more) perceive our relationship to the physical world around us.

The Judeo-Christian narrative casts God as a creator who forms the seas, the land, the animals and plants, out of nothing. (Talk about *craft*—the ultimate Maker!) In Genesis 1:28, God then makes human beings and grants them authority over all creation:

> And God said to them, be fruitful and multiply and fill the earth
> and subdue it, and have dominion over the fish of the sea and over
> the birds of the heavens and over every living thing that moves on
> the earth.

And, boom, there it is. Humans are granted primacy in the form of "dominion," which includes the right—the exhortation, even—to subdue the world around us. The earth and everything in it become objects to our subject, forever and ever, amen.

The concept of dominion has often been cited as a root cause of the waste and ecological devastation generated by Western industrial society, perhaps most famously by historian Lynn White in 1967. Trying to figure out why "no other creature other than man has ever managed to foul its nest in such short order," White pinned the blame squarely on the Judeo-Christian assumption that "God planned all of this explicitly for man's benefit and rule: no item in the physical creation had any purpose save to serve man's purposes." White traces a direct line from the biblical creation myth and concept of dominion to the development of modern science and technology, which he paints as an "out of control" destructive force for whose ecological impacts "Christianity bears a huge burden of guilt."[2]

More than sixty years later, Brian Thomas Swimme and Mary Evelyn Tucker pick up this human-centric thread in *Journey of the Universe*, a physically slim but philosophically hefty account of the cosmos and humanity's small but devastating role in it. The book asks, "What is it about our modern consciousness that enables us to avoid seeing the disastrous results of our way of life?" Like White, Tucker and Swimme point to science and technology rooted in Enlightenment thinking (which itself is rooted in Christian theology), but they get even more granular, proposing that "the destruction comes, at least in part, from an inadequate understanding of matter itself." They argue that from early Christian and medieval religious beliefs emerged a scientific and later secular body of thought that again places the human as the only meaningful center, the only subject that really matters: "Matter came to be seen as a substance devoid of subjectivity. Only humans had thought and feeling; other animals and the rest of nature operated like a machine. . . . From this modern perspective, matter exists primarily for human use. . . . Such a worldview now pervades contemporary thinking."[3]

This fundamental image of "God the Maker," and giver, of all matter places humanity at the center, the sole beneficiary of this colossal gift and subject of a vast cosmic sentence. This idea not only underlies Western religion and science but has also become codified in our system and institutions of government. The thinking that led to White's "out of control" technological forces and Swimme and Tucker's "material determinism" was also the thinking behind constitutions, bills of rights, and government structures that authoritatively presumed humanity to be at the center of creation, for better and for worse.[4]

Much of Enlightenment thinking started from the same premise as our little broken wooden plaque. John Locke based much of his work on the belief that "God, as King David says (Psalms 115:16), has given the earth to the children of men—given it to mankind in common." Locke goes further, defining very specifically the reason for this awesome gift:

"The earth and everything in it is given to men for the support and comfort of their existence." Before we condemn Locke as a piggy and exploitative anthropocentric run mad, it's important to remember that in the era in which Locke was writing, one potentially dangerous and not-uncommon reading of the biblical gift of dominion was that an absolute monarch, as God's representative on earth, might be the one charged by God to steward mankind's common gift. A pushy king could argue that "God gave the world to Adam and his successive heirs, *excluding* all the rest of his posterity,"[5] then claim himself as Adam's heir and shut out the rest of undesirable posterity. Indeed, absolute monarchs, acquisitive churches, and lots of other overeager stewards had gobbled up a lot of the earth in Locke's time. Locke reached for an interpretation of the dominion belief that would protect individual property from increasingly absolutist monarchs. One might say that Locke gave the king's subjects standing as subjects in their own right by assigning them an inalienable right to own their own objects.

Locke's era was also shaped by the movement to enclose the commons, a centuries-long process of transforming formerly shared lands into mine, yours, or his (not hers, usually). The push to enclose the commons not only expanded notions of private property but in addition shut out many of those who benefited from the commons, especially the poor. Here are the seeds of our modern middle-class notion of property—the demise of the common, a pushback against monarchy, and the rise of a system designed to protect what is *mine* that led easily to disproportionate benefits for a few.

But wait—how did we get to *mine* when the gift of the earth was explicitly given to mankind *in common*? Locke explains: "I will try to show in a positive way how men could come to own various particular parts of something that God gave to mankind in common, and how this could come about without any explicit agreement among men in general." According to Locke, that right to carve private property out of the shared whole was defensible because of the labor of the property holder. So, the water in the stream is shared, but the man who does the work to get it into the pitcher owns that particular liter of water. When a person does the work to tend, harvest, steward—or indeed exploit—our shared resources, he asserts ownership over those resources. This connection between labor and ownership is very different from other traditions, for example those of many Indigenous American cultures, where human labor did not translate to ownership over land, but rather existed in relationship with it.[6]

Because, of course, in Locke, the labor that affirmed property rights was pretty much exclusively white male labor. The labor of women and people of color also transferred ownership of the product of that labor, but not to the people who did the work, an inequity that has fueled our Western conception of dominion all the more: just as God the Maker has the right to "give" the world over to man's dominion, Man the Laborer has the right to carve out his piece of the pie and defend it. It's the foundation of a belief system based on ownership and control. And it directly feeds our current system, where amassing property, or goods, is an individual activity—a right, even—separate from and often in conflict with the common good.

Underlying our current system is Locke's argument that government *exists* to defend property, which he defined as life, liberty, and estate. This defense of property was critical in the face of the absolutism of the seventeenth century, and has been passed down to us as a fundamental role of government, and often a criterion for participation in it. In addition to race and gender, owning property (land, in this case) was one of the main requirements for suffrage in Locke's view and for centuries afterward. In the early years of the American republic, most states restricted voting rights to white male property holders. And, in an American twist, Locke's "life, health, liberty, or possessions" was adapted in the American Declaration of Independence to "Life, Liberty, and the Pursuit of

Happiness." It would not be amiss to argue that possessions and the pursuit of happiness have been muddled in the American psyche ever since.

Two Francises and Stuff

Before we pin all the blame for everything on Christian theology and its descendants, it's important to note that many, many thinkers, environmentalists, theologians, evangelicals, and everyday Christians have proposed alternative readings where dominion implies not an entitlement but an obligation. Pope Francis, another notable thinker with an inside line to the Christian god, wrote in *Laudato Si'*, his 2015 encyclical on the environment and political economy, that while "God has entrusted the world to us men and women," we have abused that trust by overstepping the boundaries of our role, and neglecting our duties as stewards: "We have come to see ourselves as her lords and masters, entitled to plunder her at will."

Francis draws a clear line between our neglect of our role as stewards and our indulgence in "the throwaway culture." While it might seem that the pope should have loftier things on his mind, and that our tendency to order new chi revitalizers rather than fix our old ones isn't at the top of the Vatican agenda, the pope makes a direct connection between the large-scale environmental challenges we face and our habits of consumption: "We have not yet managed to adopt a circular model of production capable of preserving resources for present and future generations, while limiting as much as possible the use of nonrenewable resources, moderating their consumption, maximizing their efficient use, reusing and recycling them."[7] Pope Francis goes further, decrying the habits of people in "developed countries and wealthier sectors of society, where the habit of wasting and discarding has reached unprecedented levels," and argues that our disregard for the planet is intimately linked with social inequity: "The human environment and the natural environment deteriorate together. . . . We have to realize that a true ecological approach always becomes a social approach; it must integrate questions of justice in debates on the environment, so as to hear both the cry of the earth and the cry of the poor."[8]

A much earlier Francis (of Assisi), also proposed a less damning vision for humanity's relationship with the "gift" of creation. Saint Francis, whom Lynn White called "the greatest radical in Christian history since Christ," proposed substituting the "idea of the equality of all creatures, including man, for the idea of man's limitless rule of creation." Could this radical notion extend to the physical world, as well?

Both Francises, the current pope and the long-ago saint whose name he chose, question the ideas implicit in our creation myth and explicit on the wooden sign that we fixed. Indeed, our deeply buried and unexamined feeling that "God has made these comforts for us" could use a fresh look. And funnily enough, even though we did put the sign back together again, just the act of taking off the letters and putting them back on again (or watching Michael do it—this job was on his table) opened up for me a new perspective on the role of Christianity in shaping some of my basic assumptions about the inanimate world around us. Is my stuff, much less our shared resources, really here *for me*? Do we as humans have a right to exert control over, or even to care for, the things and the world around us? Do we have an obligation to do so? Even just tuning in to these assumptions invites the question of whether there is some other model, or other sets of assumptions to consider.

Although he may have lots of influential fans, from John Locke to Pope Francis, the Judeo-Christian god is not the only one. There are many other traditions that might help us puzzle through where we stand in relation to the rest of creation—traditions that underpin systems of belief and consumption around the globe. Providentially, a few additional objects helped point me toward some of those other modes of thinking about God and stuff.

Seven Bhagavad Gitas and Lots of Diapers: The Art and Religion of Maintenance

The count of Hindu gods ranges from 11—or 33, or 33 million—to as many as 330 million, and there are countless stories about these multiple deities collected in numerous texts. So perhaps it is fitting that to draw our attention to this religion of rich multiplicity, I can report that we received and fixed not one but seven copies of the Bhagavad Gita over the course of our pop-ups. All of them were brought to us by Amla, a dedicated customer and Inwood neighbor of Indian descent. In addition to her Bhagavad Gitas, Amla also brought us, over the years, several necklaces, a Waterpik, a couple of lamps, a set of window blinds, a wallet, and some delicious Indian snacks (to eat, not to fix). Amla enjoyed our shops and supported us with her business, her cooking, and her encouragement over the years. But she was not shy about declining our services when she thought the price was too high and the object was small enough. In those instances, especially if she had a trip coming up, she would simply take the broken object with her to India and have it fixed there.

Amla described a multiplicity of fixers available in Mumbai, from tailors skilled at reweaving holes in clothes to specialists in audio equipment. She indicated, however, that these traditional occupations are in decline and that in her experience in India, as here, fixers are becoming less common as the price of new goods goes down. Other repair options (like the Indian startup UrbanClap, somewhat akin to the home services site TaskRabbit) are trying to pull repair into the twenty-first-century market. So while Indian patterns of consumption seem to be subject to many of the same forces as American ones, I wondered if some of the core beliefs of Hinduism might provide a different perspective.

The first main difference is the conception of the relationship between a god or gods, the earth, and humans. O. P. Dwivedi wrote that in the Mahabharata, "this universe and every object in it has been created as an abode of the Supreme God; it is meant for the benefit of all; individual species must therefore learn to enjoy its benefits by existing as part of a system, in close relationship with other species and without permitting any one species to encroach upon the others' rights."[9]

In the Bible, God creates the earth: it is separate, an object that you can almost imagine God holding in his hands. In this Hindu version, there is less separation between God and Creation; the two are intertwined or can even be seen as one thing: "Actually, mountains are his bones, earth is the flesh, sea is the blood, and sky is his abdomen. The sun and moon are his eyes. The upper part of the sky is his head, the earth is his feet, and directions are his hands."[10] This idea of the earth as the body of God breaks down the subject-object relationship, creating a different understanding of what we are doing when we damage the environment—we are not just breaking an object we were given but harming the gods themselves.

It's important to remember that Hinduism is a religion rich with a multiplicity of stories, texts, interpretations. When I ran this conception of the earth as the body of God by Amla (who owns all those Bhagavad Gitas because she is working on a new translation), she smiled and said, "Well, that's possible! Hinduism is complex."[11] There is more than one way to read the myths, to understand the stories, and many ways to practice. One core belief of Hinduism, however, is the idea of the main trinity of Brahma, Shiva, and Vishnu. These gods are also complex, but in simplest terms, Brahma is the creator god, Shiva is the destroyer, and Vishnu is the preserver or protector.

Vishnu is often cited as the most important of the three, with many forms. He protects and restores when the world is thrown out of balance: he preserves, sustains, maintains. The primacy of this god in Hinduism—the god of maintenance—contrasts with the Christian tradition, which gives preference to God the Maker (and sometimes God the Destroyer). The Christian tradition places a very high value on creating and a relatively low value on maintaining, preserving, restoring balance. As evidence of the high value Judeo-Christian America places on creation, witness our obsession with innovation, our recurring passion for the newest technology, the primacy of making in our mythology and in our economic system (remember the Zane Grey plate), and our angst as that identity as a nation of makers has declined.

But what about Vishnu? What about maintenance? Western society doesn't really have a name for this form of power. God the Maker, God the Destroyer, God the . . . Fixer? Sustaining, maintaining, and preserving are not highly valued in the West. In basic, financial terms, it's hard to fund maintenance (just look at the New York subway) because it's not "sexy"; that is to say, it's not seen as valuable or instrumental. Maintenance is seen as a form of obligatory "catch-up" rather than powerful and constructive mutual interdependence. The people in our society who perform maintenance and care and stewardship are regularly paid less than others. On average, maintenance workers and caregivers earn about eleven dollars an hour, at least ten dollars less than the average hourly wage in the United States.[12] It's hard to fund maintenance, very simply, because we don't value it highly in our society, and that cultural attitude is reflected in the prices we assign to it.

The low status of maintenance is also clear when you are trying to pay repair shop fixers a living wage. In our first shop, we paid our fixers (including ourselves) $100 per day, which basically meant asking a favor of our theatre colleagues, who could earn more than that downtown on a show. By 2016, we managed to raise the rate to fifteen dollars per hour, and finally got up to twenty dollars—a big lift given how lean our business had to run, but still difficult for someone trying to make a living in New York City. Our hourly rates for fixers, however, were constrained by how much customers were willing to pay for the maintenance and upkeep of their stuff. As we've seen, people were willing to spend more than what we had anticipated, because of their emotional attachments to shower radios and lamps and Bhagavad Gitas, but at an average price of forty dollars per repair, it was a challenge to pay our fixers a rate we felt was commensurate with the skill involved. We felt keenly the invisibility, and relatively low value, of this type of work.

That same year, I took my students to see an exhibit at the Queens Museum, a retrospective of the work of the artist Mierle Laderman Ukeles. Ukeles's extraordinary body of work documents, exposes, and elevates what she calls "maintenance art," the unseen and unlauded work of cleaning, fixing, sanitation, and housework. To document and elevate the work of maintenance, Ukeles took pictures of urinals. She scrubbed the steps of public buildings. She washed sanitary napkins in a toilet. She choreographed large-scale ballets of public vehicles like bulldozers and garbage trucks. She took Polaroids of workers mopping offices. Over a period of eleven months in 1979–80, she shook hands with every sanitation worker in the city of New York. Her work made visible the unseen and underpaid labor of caring for that which already exists.

Ukeles wrote a manifesto in 1969, in which she identifies two basic systems of work: Development and Maintenance. She saw our society as giving primacy to Development, while neglecting and devaluing maintenance: "The culture confers lousy status on maintenance jobs = minimum wages, housewives = no pay."[13] Her Polaroids and handshakes and bulldozer ballets were an attempt to document that devalued work and the people—largely women and people of color—who do it: "The manifesto is also a call for the full-scale reorganization of society: for Maintenance to be valued and for Development to be seriously questioned. Women have been society's traditional maintainers, and this was clearly a feminist statement. But it was also a call for an alliance with men who maintain—to forge a coalition across lines of both gender and class."[14]

Ukeles explicitly linked the devaluation of this individual labor with the overall, global devaluation of stewardship. In 1969, she created a proposal for an exhibition called *Care*, which addressed "Personal, Societal/

Urban, and Planetary Maintenance," and sent it to several museums and institutions. The proposal was rejected. Ukeles was ahead of her time.

Valuing the Gods of Maintenance, at Home

I was very moved by the Ukeles exhibit. Not only was I deep in the trenches of repairing people's broken stuff, a highly devalued and unglamorous type of work, but her perspective on motherhood and maintenance also struck a chord. I remember when I was a young(er) fool, I used to rail against "maintenance." I declared that one could spend one's entire life just maintaining things, instead of "actually living." You could spend all week, all month, all year, just balancing checkbooks, cleaning up, making the bed, getting haircuts, going to the doctor and dentist for checkups, straightening up, and, yes, I suppose repairing stuff. Those were things my mother did (she is a maintenance virtuoso), but which in my younger years I cavalierly dismissed as a distraction from the "real" work of making things, new things.

My whole being was centered on the goal of creating new designs; that is, making new stuff, mainly scenery for theatre. It felt important to me to make new things, to create out of nothing, and I poured a huge amount of energy into it. I made scenic flats that would be used once out of lauan, a hardwood chopped down in virgin forests in Asia. I made costumes for such eminently important productions as *Wuthering Heights: The Musical.* I hauled stuff around the city in bags and boxes and U-Hauls, all so that I could make even more stuff. And once it was made, I walked away—my job was done. A designer doesn't have to maintain the design, and we don't have to take it apart when the show is over. Our job is to dream, to imagine, to create from scratch, like God the Maker. And this felt right to me; I thought it was real work, valuable work.

Like Ukeles, when I did finally make something that I couldn't walk away from—namely, a baby—my conception of work, my understanding of what was important in this world, my opinions on maintenance (and basically, my point of view on just about everything) changed. One reason for this is that caring for a baby felt to me like 110 percent maintenance work. If the birth was the glorious act of creation, the fabulous opening night, then the days that followed were filled with a strange mundanity that much of the world—and until then I myself—had deemed insignificant. There were tiny nails to be kept trimmed, rashy butts to be swabbed, little clothes to be washed and folded and sorted, doctor checkups until you are blue in the face. For someone who was used to charging around in the professional world, doing "important" things, these small acts of maintenance felt, like the work Ukeles sought to document, invisible and unimportant. They were certainly unremunerated.

But slowly I came to see that the endless work of caring for a baby—of maintaining, preserving, and protecting—while perhaps unglamorous and certainly underpaid in our economy, all adds up to what, for a young mother, feels like the most important thing in the whole wide world: a happy, healthy baby with a reasonably dry butt who can smile at you and change your life. All the previous charging around that I had done, making new scenery, now seemed utterly pointless. Caring for—maintaining—this little creature felt important, and my eyes were opened to the value—or as Ukeles might put it, the art—of maintenance.

The Chi Revitalizer

If Amla's Bhagavad Gitas plus a visit to the Queens Museum helped articulate the importance of recognizing and valuing maintenance as much as we do creation, the chi revitalizer helped introduce another philosophical approach to repair and stuff.

You might think that a "chi revitalizer" sounds like a joke—or maybe a typo. I wasn't at our greenmarket stand the snowy December day

Cynthia dropped it off, but I saw it listed in our database and was mystified. In case you are confused, too, a chi revitalizer is a little machine, sort of like a footstool that plugs in. You rest your ankles on the padded stool, and it shakes your legs gently back and forth. The motion rebalances, or I suppose revitalizes, your chi (or qi): your "vital energy," your "life force." The machine was not working at all. To fix it, Adam removed the frayed cord, shortened it, and rewired the machine. As it turns out, chi revitalizers are fairly pricey ($274.95 on Amazon), so Cynthia was thrilled when we managed to get it swinging again for only forty dollars.

I have to admit that there was a bit of slightly unprofessional hilarity in the shop on the day Adam fixed the chi revitalizer. Not everyone was convinced that this machine's promised benefits were legit, plus we looked goofy testing it out to make sure it worked. It seemed a little ludicrous—a jiggling, plug-in footstool impacting your life force, your vital energy? There are a lot of people out there on the internet with a lot of things to say about chi machines (as on any topic), some of it too good to be believed: "This thing is amazing. It's sent my usually sluggish and tired energy soaring! It's calmed my ravenous appetite! It's lessened the intensity and frequency of my almost daily headaches!" Despite the occasional hyperbole, a lot of people swear by it. Maybe the chi revitalizer might have something to teach us, after all. In the words of Pope Francis, "Who am I to judge?"

Chi, or qi, is a concept threaded through Confucianism and Daoist traditions. It's a life force, an energy that exists across the universe and in each of us. Chi "is seen as creating the movement and reciprocity of the universe, being the basis of the interaction and continuation of life, the spontaneous arising and decaying of things." This philosophy places humans *within* the workings of nature, not somehow separate from them or immune to them. The earth is not an object to be created or managed. In fact, "there is no creation and no external creator God or heaven to be sought, rather, the universe is complete unto itself," and we are part of the whole. Perhaps this de-objectification of the world around us allows Daoists to "value the capacity for self-transformation that is inherent within things."[15]

Thinking this way can be a shift. Rather than seeing the broken chi revitalizer as a problem, a bit of creation to be managed, perhaps it is just a natural phase in the life cycle of one of the "ten thousand things," the Daoist conception of all the myriad things we "name," or see as separate, as objects. Following this line of thinking, if each object has its own path, you might wonder, why fix it at all? Just let the thing continue on its journey. Daoism, however, does find a role for humans in "good and bad ways of channeling qi, causing harmony and growth or disorder and destruction," ideally serving as an agent of "cosmic transformation," nurturing change and harmony, but not seeking to control.[16]

This view of repair is appealing. We in the shop always knew that the "product" we turned out was not a chi revitalizer (or blender, or chair) that was made "new," but rather a chi revitalizer that, through our inter-action with it, was able to head back out into the flow of the cosmos, or at least the flow of Cynthia's life, and continue to do its thing for a while longer. We know the chi revitalizer won't last forever—our job is simply to care for it briefly, to help it find a path that for a while at least does not lead to the dump.

A Bench with Low Self-Esteem

This perspective of the object's having its own journey, its own des-tiny, and that we simply crossed its path for a while may sound a little cuckoo, but since this seems to be the appropriate chapter for confes-sion, I have to admit that it was a concept already intuitively familiar to me. I will cop to a habit (which I have also observed in other designers) of taking into consideration the point of view of a piece of furniture—in other words, trying to "hear" what the furniture is saying in the context of the larger play and the other "texts" being spoken.

When looking for the perfect placement of a piece of set dressing or a prop, there are many considerations: Will the fire curtain smash onto the object in the case of a fire? Is the object close enough to the table so that the actor can get to it before his monologue runs out? Is the object too bright in contrast to the wall behind it? And on and on.

But in creating a stage picture—which, as a reminder, is much more than a picture, but is rather a world, a set of "thematic signifiers"[17]—it is also useful to tune in to the actual objects themselves. I remember a design meeting for a show I designed, somewhere between pop-ups nine and ten. We were trying to figure out what type of furniture we needed for the production, and I expressed the desire to make sure we avoided benches and chairs "with low self-esteem." The director laughed heartily. But I was being serious, so I paused to consider what I actually meant.

Imagine life from the bench's perspective. Benches are the humble workhorses of theatrical sittables. They are big enough to accommodate two people, but usually light enough to be moved by one. They are highly functional and often relatively simple visually, so they can move easily between different scenes or spaces. They get painted, stood on, kicked over, and generally worked to death, and then they go back to a dusty shelf in the prop warehouse to wait for their next gig. But what does the bench want, if anything? When I walk through the furniture storage rooms, choosing the lucky items like some sort of powerful deity in the prop pantheon, I always imagine that they want to get out of storage and get onstage, they want a chance to shine a little bit, to contribute to the scene.

So sometimes I think about the bench that I want or need, or that will best fit the play, or serve the actor's needs best. But it can also be fun to listen to what the *bench* wants in order to find the best furniture for the show. Does this particular bench want to join the show, but it needs a new coat of paint, or reupholstery to fit in? Does it want the part but really isn't a good fit? Is it just too big, or too rickety? The kinds of low-self-esteem benches I was referring to are, sadly, the ones that have been so beat up, painted so many times, reinforced with angle irons, and generally abused by theatre folk that they no longer remember what it means to be a real bench, rather than looking like generic "theatre" furniture just one step up from a rehearsal cube. It's a sad fate, but it happens, and those benches should perhaps be put out to pasture.

In hearing (or, yes, I know, maybe imagining) what the bench wants, in addition to actually hearing "out loud" what the fire marshal and the actor and the lighting designer want, I begin to understand the objects in our world as subjects, as well. This propensity may seem strange, or of limited utility to someone whose paycheck does not depend on choosing the right bench, but our perspective on the things around us matters a lot. Sometimes it takes a drastic shift in perspective to see how, and why. Imagining life from the point of view of a bench is one way; one writer took a more adventurous route.

Beyond the Stuff of Organized Religion

I've been using Michael Pollan's work on food as a helpful guide for how we can think about stuff, and we've seen how he flipped the script on corn and other plants colonizing *us*. But I was surprised to find that he has some thoughts on the subject-object relationship beyond plants. As Pollan discovered in a yearslong exploration, both intellectual and personal, of LSD, mushrooms, ayahuasca, and other mind-altering drugs,

> One of the gifts of psychedelics is the way they reanimate the world, as if they were distributing the blessings of consciousness more widely and evenly over the landscape, in the process breaking the human monopoly on subjectivity we moderns take as a given. To us,

we are the world's only conscious subjects, with the rest of creation made up of objects; to the more egotistical among us, even other people count as objects. Psychedelic consciousness overturns that view, by granting us a wider, more generous lens through which we can glimpse the subject-hood—the spirit!—of everything, animal, vegetable, even mineral, all of it now somehow returning our gaze.[18]

Even if you don't have the opportunity to smoke toad venom, it is possible to tap into the subject-hood of things simply by spending many years listening closely to them, as you work with them to create a world, and to see them, and the actor and the lights, the stage and all the players in it, as a "densely tangled web of subjects, each acting on the other in the great dance."[19]

And perhaps cultivating an ability to see the interconnectedness of it all—even worn-out benches, wooden plaques, tattered books, and broken chi revitalizers—will help us rethink a few things. Set designers (and prop masters, and artists, and people who make things a lot, and perhaps Marie Kondo) may be more in tune with the subjects inside our objects than others are, but we all have this capacity to some degree or another. The emotional tug we feel when we throw out something "perfectly good" is another way of granting, or perceiving, the subject-hood of the thing. The simple phrasing, heard when moving into a new apartment: "Where does the couch want to live?" indicates that we can see the objects around us communicating, as players in the story.

In acknowledging the potential for independent perspective in a thing, or the ten thousand things, in sharing the limelight however temporarily, we perceive and at least briefly acknowledge the interconnectedness of all things. This, in turn, might just help open the door to a new model that contextualizes our needs more carefully with those of other people, animals, and even things: a model where we acknowledge the deep value of maintenance, preservation, and care.

PART V

PASS IT ON

What happens at the end?

Even if you've bought durable, high-quality stuff and taken care of it well, there does sometimes come the moment when you need to get rid of something. Either you are done with it for one good reason or another, or the object itself has truly reached the end of its useful life. In both these cases, it's necessary—and possible—to find ways to "pass it on," either to another user or another manufacturing process, so that the materials can be reclaimed and made into something new. Finding a home for something useful when you are done with it is one of the final and critical elements of a circular system.

In this final step, we will examine some of the ways to facilitate such a cycle on an individual and systemic level, some current barriers to recirculating goods and reclaiming materials, and a few of the many companies and practices that are making it easier for us to pass it on.

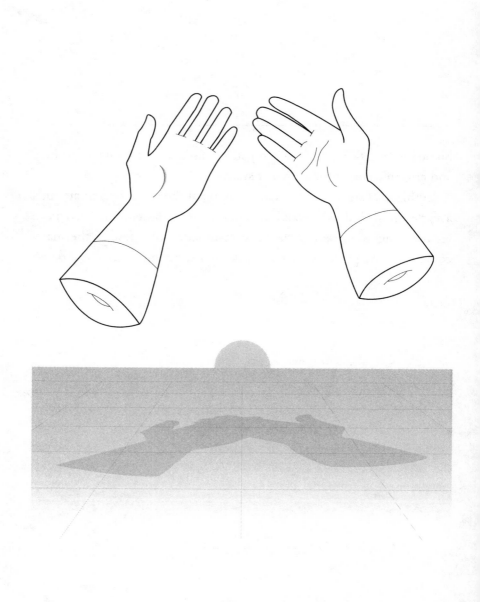

CHAPTER 9:

From Cradle to Grave

When I lost my keys you told me the words of Plato
That our possessions are only shadows, echoes of fate, so
The things that you lose, you never possessed,
You're only remembering,
Only remembering.
And all we see is stars,
Falling from so far away;
The things that we see are just memories of the
Things that used to be.
—"Stars," music and lyrics by Michael Friedman

About the time of our third pop-up, my grandmother passed away. She'd had a stroke a few years earlier and died in her sleep one night in January 2014 at the age of ninety-four. Amid the sadness, and the celebrations of her long and fruitful life, came the inevitable coping with her houseful of rather huge amounts of stuff. My grandmother had five children, four husbands, lots of pets, a big house, and a generous and dignified demeanor. She also had a tendency to accumulate. She had lived in the same house since 1949, a long and low split-level Norman-style house with several bedrooms, designed by my inveterate inventor/tinkerer/fixer/stuff-genius grandfather. While she was nowhere near hoarder territory, the nooks and crannies of her house were always full of exciting treasures for a grandchild: the coin collection glued to a dresser in the downstairs bedroom, boxes of handkerchiefs hand-embroidered with old-fashioned family names like Crampton, crumbling books about steam shovels, a flat white box labeled *Mimi's lorgnette* in thin slanted cursive (Mimi was my great-great-grandmother), an old leather megaphone that brought to mind college football games and raccoon coats, and a remote control with just three big buttons that changed the TV channel with a satisfyingly significant *click*.

I remember the desk where Nana would make phone calls, always seated with her eyes closed, a habit that seemed to belong to an earlier era, when a telephone call demanded one's full attention. She sat surrounded by piles of papers, cards, and newspaper clippings, somewhat sorted and awaiting distribution to the correct relatives. Her philosophy toward stuff was perhaps summed up by a clipping above the desk that read A CLEAN DESK IS THE SIGN OF A SICK MIND.

Toward the end of her life, however, Nana seemed reluctant to leave unattended the piles of papers, the closets full of vintage clothes, and the attic full of relics. She did not want to leave her children with the task of sorting it all, and slowly, bit by bit, she worked through as much of it as she could; she figured out what to give away (and how), what to pass on to family, and what had to go to the trash. My grandmother took upon herself the difficult process of closing out her life in stuff.

Our lives are marked with stuff, from the cradle to the grave. We are born, and right away we are showered with onesies and blankets and squeaky giraffes. Each birthday is marked by more gifts: Legos and stamp sets, and later on tablets and gift cards. We go to college and squeeze our belongings into a tiny dorm room, or we commute to campus and try to launch adult lives from a childhood room. We get married and find ways to merge our stuff—commingling old books on shelves, choosing new things together. We get divorced and have to reverse that process, returning again to "yours" and "mine." And when we come to the end, either we or our loved ones face the work of figuring out what to do with the physical record of who we were.

Even though Nana worked hard to sort through her stuff toward the end, there was a great deal still left in the house after she passed. It was amazing, and also quite beautiful, to go through some of it. To see the little printed tags with her children's names on them in her (many) sewing boxes and drawers, to imagine her carefully stitching them onto summer camp blankets and T-shirt collars. I found at least five or six lovely wooden darning eggs, along with delicate scissors, numerous thimbles, and button replacement kits from hotels where she had stayed in the 1960s. I had never thought of my grandmother as much of a "handy" person—I don't remember ever seeing her sew, but there was the record of many years of mending, labeling, and stitching.

As the family sorted and sifted through furniture and pictures and dishware and more, I took an old sewing box and several of the darning eggs and thread snips. These items seemed useful as well as beautiful, and I liked the idea of rescuing her tools from their drawers and using them again in our shops. However, there were many, many items of Nana's that we weren't able to find a home for, that the thrift stores wouldn't take, and that ultimately wound up in a landfill.

The Toddler Bed: Barriers to Circularity

Much of my grandmother's stuff wound up in the landfill because of economic, logistical, and psychological barriers in our culture today. That may sound like a fancy way of saying nobody wanted or needed most of her stuff, but it's worth pausing to figure out why that is the case, especially since the phenomenon of "unneeded stuff" is relatively new. For centuries, people's wills specified the destination of not only money but also goods such as clothing, furniture, sheets, table linens, and the like. To get to a healthier pattern of consumption, to complete the cycle and close the loop, we've got to get used to passing things on again, and we've got to make the practice easier, more popular, and more expected.

One major barrier, as discussed previously, is the low price of new goods. As long as the social costs of manufacturing wages overseas, the artificially low cost of raw materials, and the environmental costs of shipping things all over the globe using fossil fuels remain unaccounted for, we have an artificial downward pressure on prices. It's a tall order to change these things, but there are signs of progress: increasing awareness of North American and international fair trade certification standards; the recent move by some companies to include factors other than just shareholder returns in their bottom line;[1] the growing push by individuals toward conscious consumption; positive regulatory and legal movements incentivizing and protecting sustainability and stewardship; and the changes in design approaches resulting in an explosion of products made from reclaimed materials. Each of these factors is part of a fast-growing stuff movement that will ultimately lead to higher prices for new stuff, additional revenue streams from reuse and repair for manufacturers and retailers, and alternative forms of "ownership," such as rental models and sharing economies. For now, however, new goods are still cheap and plentiful, which makes it much harder to find homes for old stuff.

And there are other barriers to "passing it on" that should also be addressed. First is the lack of incentives, or worse, counterincentives. In New York City today, for example, I have absolutely zero incentive to do anything other than toss something once I am done with it.

My younger son, who was a baby at our first pop-up, recently outgrew his toddler bed and graduated to a loft bed built by Michael. The white IKEA toddler bed had been given to us by our neighbors, so we felt karmically okay in terms of how we got it in the first place, and I wanted to try to keep it in circulation. We had already had a very hard time getting rid of his crib, which was itself a hand-me-down from my sister. No one seemed to want a twice-used crib even though it was really in fine shape, and after trying valiantly for several months to find a good home for it, we wound up dropping it at a local thrift store, which is always a bit of a crapshoot.

Thrift stores are increasingly overwhelmed by stuff, often selling in bulk overseas or dumping the excess into landfills. Donations are up; perhaps people have become frustrated with peak stuff, or are inspired by Marie Kondo to tidy up, or are donating their old stuff to some abstract person in need to try to assuage their climate guilt. The uncomfortable fact of the matter, however, is that while donating to those in need is admirable, it's not enough. People at the middle and high ends of the economic spectrum need to start buying a lot more used goods of all kinds. Donating alone doesn't cut it—it does not reliably close the loop.[2]

For the toddler bed, I was determined to do better. I tried to post it on AptDeco, but the value was too low; since AptDeco charges for delivery, it has a minimum price per item, and I didn't think anyone would spend $100 on my used toddler bed, especially since a comparable new one on IKEA cost less than that. I tried Craigslist, posting it for twenty dollars, and got a few responses, but each sale fell through. The weeks went by and the bed sat disassembled in a corner of the living room, bothering me like the un-crossed-off to-do item that it was. Finally I posted on Facebook Marketplace and got a couple of responses, one of which was from a neighbor around the corner, a young man we knew from the local barbershop. He came by that same afternoon and I helped walk the bed over to his apartment, where it would serve as a double bed for his two dogs. In all, I spent about two months trying to pass on that toddler bed. I know it is unreasonable to expect people who are not writing books about consumption to devote that much time to "rehoming" a used IKEA bed. As the countless desks, chairs, beds, and other items I see in the trash on NYC streets attest, it's much easier to just put it in the trash.

In addition to the inconvenience of passing things on, the economic incentives are backward. In New York, for example, our taxes pay for the sanitation department to come haul away our bags of waste, our recycling, and our large items like toddler beds. But this is a sunk cost that has no influence on my behavior—I pay the same taxes whether I spend two months finding German shepherds to live on my kid's stuff or just dump it on the curb.

Some municipalities have introduced a "pay as you throw" (PAYT) model, where households pay according to how much trash they generate, a policy that has been shown to reduce the volume of trash collected and improve recycling rates. The power of economic incentives cannot be overstated. In Ireland, a fifteen-cent bag fee led within weeks to a 94 percent reduction in plastic bag use. South Korea increased composting 93 percent by charging a fee per pound for residential waste. If it had cost me twenty-five dollars to have my toddler bed hauled, the way it does in some areas of the country, the incentive for me to find a new home for it would be much greater, and it starts being worth the time.[3]

For people who are willing and have the time to make a bit of an effort right now, without waiting for their city or state to change the incentive structure, there are ways to make passing things on easier. There are online marketplaces, including Letgo, OfferUp, AptDeco, good old Craigslist, Facebook Marketplace, and many more. There are also more informal "curb alerts" and other online or community systems; one Instagram page in New York is called Stooping NYC (@ stoopingnyc), where you can post and find used things on the street.[4]

There are important steps that cities and municipalities could take to support these types of platforms as part of a strategy to get to zero waste. PAYT models are clearly effective. Concentrating a neighborhood's bulk pickups on certain clearly posted days of the week can make curb alerts more effective. And clear and convenient pickups or drop-off events for specialty items can help too. The bottom line is that we should— must—continue to build, support, and incentivize systems that make it easier to pass things on. Otherwise, we are relying on people to voluntarily devote their time and effort and lose money in the process—and that's a losing proposition.

Lots of Printers and Other Repair Fails

There are, however, instances where passing items on to another user is not possible or not realistic. There are times when an object reaches the end of its useful life, when it doesn't make sense to pass it on to another person, but rather it should be fed back into the system of manufacture.

Printers were a recurring source of stress for us in our shops, for several reasons. First, people brought them fairly often. Second, they were unpredictable—hard to diagnose, hard to test, difficult to find parts for, and liable to suck up a lot of a fixer's time. As such, they were hard for us to estimate good prices for; a job might take twenty minutes, as when we fished out a cupful of bobby pins and an Uno card from Jean F.'s printer and were able to get it working again; or it might take three hours and still result in a repair fail. Of the many broken printers people brought to us, parts were unavailable for most of them, and in the end only a few were successfully fixed.

For items like printers, or anything that plugged in, we charged our customers a twenty-dollar diagnostic fee to cover the time spent opening the machine, downloading software drivers, figuring out if ink tanks were empty, and so on. If the repair failed, it didn't seem right to ask them to come pick up their (unfixed) printer, so we started offering "responsible disposal" for repair fails. This meant that at the end of each pop-up, we were stuck with a sorry collection of small appliances, printers, and other electronics.

The options for responsible disposal are limited. Is there even such a thing as responsible disposal, if the recycling rate for electronics globally is only 16 percent? For residential pickup in New York and many other municipalities, residents can now put kitchen appliances and e-waste out for pickup, or can participate in drop-off events. Items like these are taken to e-recycling locations, where they are shredded into metal, glass, and plastic.[5] In theory, all the materials are reclaimed. Unfortunately, upwards of 130 e-recyclers in the United States have been "fined, abandoned, gone bankrupt, or been caught exporting e-scrap to developing countries."[6] BAN, Basel Action Network, is a nonprofit focused on halting the transfer of hazardous e-waste from developed countries to poorer areas. In a 2016 report, BAN tracked "recycled" e-waste and found that "40 percent did not get recycled in the US as expected by customers, but were instead exported to highly-polluting and unsafe operations in developing countries—mostly in Asia."[7]

If e-waste alone is so complicated, the prospect of responsibly rehoming a whole household's worth of stuff, like my grandmother's, can be truly daunting and can make outsourcing very appealing. Companies like Junkluggers, for example, will sort through your stuff, resell and recycle what they can, and trash the rest. While the company aims to have very little of what they collect wind up in landfill, they estimate that "about 25 percent of the stuff we try to recycle is too contaminated to go anywhere but the landfill." And that's the stuff people were willing to pay someone to come lug away.[8] There are also more informal salvage economies in many parts of the country, where certain items (air conditioners, transformers, other electronics) are reclaimed and stripped for valuable materials like copper.[9]

The ideal is a system where 100 percent of the materials in an object are reclaimed. For this to happen, designers would have to design for not only repair but eventual dismantling of objects, too—no more monstrous hybrids. They'd also have to design new products that are made with reclaimed materials, because until there is a market for these materials, the systems for reclaiming them won't grow.

A few companies are already building completely circular models for their own goods, designing products with materials that already exist. For Days makes T-shirts from recycled cotton, which is reclaimed from used products that its customers return to the company. Nothing New sneakers are made from just that: nothing new. Patagonia introduced a "recrafted" line of jackets and bags made from old jackets and bags. Apart from these companies on the leading edge, most brands, as we saw with Andy's iPad, don't go beyond vaguely encouraging customers to "recycle" their products. But since the actual amount of reclaimed materials in their new products is relatively low, or more often next to nothing, the loop remains decidedly open.

Closing the Loop

Witnessing the end of my grandmother's life while fixing (and sometimes failing to fix) so many objects made me think about the parallels between the way we treat our bodies at the end of our lives and the way we treat our stuff. In some ways, our current inability to reclaim the materials in the stuff we make mimics the linear system we have created for our own bodies. We bury or incinerate our stuff, and we bury or incinerate ourselves. We are the only animals on earth whose bodies, when we die, do not feed back into another nutrient cycle of one kind or another. We fill our bodies with embalming chemicals, and place them in heavy metal coffins, doing everything we can to deny the process of decay and reabsorption into another life-form. It's a strange approach to the end of life, and one we have replicated for many of the objects that mark and define our lives as well.

My grandmother was cremated, and we sprinkled her ashes at the beach where she spent almost every summer of her life. That was her wish, and typical for her era. By the time I go, however, I hope that the stuff that makes me—in body and home—will somehow find a way back into circulation: my stuff absorbed into someone else's home and life the way Nana's darning eggs were absorbed into our repair shop's tool kits, and my body into the swirl of nutrients that cycle through our planet's natural systems.

CONCLUSION:

Fight for It

"You don't have to be one of those people that accepts things as they are. Every day, take responsibility for changing them right where you are."
—Cory Booker

On my way home from the subway, I walk along one of the main commercial streets of my neighborhood. Banks and chain pharmacies dominate the prime corner locations, while sneaker stores, barbershops, and 99¢ stores dot the interior stretches of each block. Many of these stores are filled with racks and shelves stacked to the fluorescent lights with air fresheners, toilet plungers, plastic pistols, polyester nightgowns, decorative coat hooks, jumbo cans of flavored popcorn, elasticized hip-slimming girdles. Products are also arrayed out front, on racks or folding tables crowded with tank tops, bath mats, shower curtains, underwear, plastic slippers.

These storefront displays are complemented by a rich variety of street vendors' wares: carts holding pastelitos, juice, or ices, or card tables loaded with dolls with arms and legs that move, tiny plastic radios, fake aquariums. On the edge of the sidewalk, yet another series of items are laid out on blankets in front of open car trunks. The blankets are populated by all kinds of used goods: shoes, phone chargers, drills, glass pie plates. Finally, around the corners on the side streets, the humblest items are offered out of black plastic shopping bags, usually clothing but also things like toilet seats or ancient flip-phone chargers. I navigate this teeming, layered ecosystem of stuff as I walk home from the subway.

One day on my train ride home, I read a *New York Times* article about falling bug populations worldwide, as illustrated by German insect populations that have declined by 75 percent over a quarter century. I had recently finished Elizabeth Kolbert's *Sixth Extinction*, so the bug bad news was just another layer of shocking and painful statistics: "One-third of all reef-building corals, a third of all freshwater mollusks, a third of all sharks and rays, a quarter of all mammals, a fifth of all reptiles, and a sixth of all birds are headed toward oblivion."[1] As I looked up from the scrolling tales of devastation on my phone, I emerged from the train, descended from the elevated platform, and dived into the massive stream of toys and shoes and toilet seat covers that mark my way home.

As I walked, I imagined the amazing process of transformation that brought those items to my street, and to millions of other streets and stores around the world. Each colorful plush toy represents, in some way, the matter and energy of a living plant or animal transformed into plastic or cloth, reshaped into a mute simulacrum of life, and displayed for us to move through, like human clownfish on some sort of strange plastic reef. Each pound of fossil fuels burned to bring that plush toy to my neighborhood represents the accumulated, disintegrated life of creatures that lived millions of years ago. Our mass extinction, the drastic global decline in species of all kinds, can actually be seen as a massive planetwide transformation of biomass: from plants and wildlife into farmed food, grass—and stuff.

We are transforming the earth into an object of our own creation. Humans make up less than 0.01 percent of the planet's biomass, but human activity has led to the reduction of the biomass of wild mammals by a factor of six, and cut plant matter by half.[2] Much of this transformation is into food—the biomass of cattle and pigs is now more than fourteen times that of all wild mammals.[3]

Some of the transformation, however, reshapes biomass into what might be called "stuffomass." It's hard to calculate exactly how much stuff humans make every year, but in 2018 we traded more than $19 trillion worth of goods around the world.[4] To give a sense of what that means in terms of stuffomass, 9.5 million twenty-foot container units entered the Los Angeles container port in 2018—and that is just one port. But really, the evidence is all around us. The volume of goods in any one given superstore is mind-boggling; just try to multiply that in your head by every store in every town, every city. It's starkly, almost pathetically evident at many zoos, where we watch one irate lonely animal pace an enclosure and read a sign about the 500 WILD SIBERIAN TIGERS left alive in the wild, and then exit through a gift shop that has five hundred stuffed toy Siberian tigers on display.

It's evident as I walk home on a concrete street teeming with human beings maneuvering through stacks and piles and racks and bags of manufactured goods—but almost entirely devoid of any other forms of life. The piles of stuff I encounter on my short walk home are, as Dr. Seuss says, so big and so tall, and above all so unnecessary (how many capri leggings could one neighborhood need?), that it seems impossible to see our human drive to make things as anything other than out of control. We are quite literally transforming the natural world into a manufactured one, populated not with bugs and animals and *life* but with a grotesque facsimile of it: T-shirts with butterflies on them, stuffed polar bears, plastic figurines of nearly extinct animals of all kinds.

About thirteen thousand years ago, a human being carved a piece of mammoth tusk into the shape of a swimming reindeer. It's the third-oldest item chronicled in Neil MacGregor's *History of the World in 100 Objects*, and the first object that is not clearly utilitarian. (The first two are stone hand axes.)[5] MacGregor's epic history through stuff implies that first, we made tools, presumably for eating. Then, sated, we very soon began to use those tools to re-create the world around us. The reindeer sculpture may have been symbolic or decorative or religious; we don't know. But it is clear that very early in our history we developed the compulsion to transform the animate world into inanimate objects. Today, walking down the street from my subway stop, through any mall, or through any zoo gift shop, we see that the impulse—the need—to represent the world around us has reached a frenzied scale and pace that are draining the reefs, the forests, and the skies.

Saving the World, with a Puffy Jacket and a Toaster

We opened our first repair shop in 2013, more than six years ago. I started rethinking the way I shop and the way I design more than ten years ago. Over those ten years, the tenor of conversation about the environment in this country has changed drastically, as has the subset of conversations about consumption. In many ways, it's gotten worse: more dire warnings from scientists, more real-world devastation from Puerto Rico to Australia and everywhere in between, more impacts on communities that are the most vulnerable, more inaction or mis-action by our national government. In a few small ways, it's gotten better. Despite the rise of Trump, Bolsonaro, Morrison, and other leaders who seem determined to do as much environmental damage as possible, there is now at least a widespread acceptance that climate change is real, and that it is affecting people right now, right here and everywhere, most especially those with the fewest resources to cope with it. This basic understanding, while still not unanimous, is something that six years ago felt nearly impossible.

There has also been a significant shift in the conversation about solutions. From a stuff guru's perspective, one way to illustrate this difference is by looking at the outdoor gear company Patagonia. Over the years, the company's initiatives have been on the leading edge of a broader cultural evolution in our approach to overconsumption in the context of the climate crisis.

From the start, Patagonia was an eco-conscious company, supporting nonprofits and raising awareness of environmental issues. In the early 1990s, the company realized that it needed to get its own "house in order,"[6] and began to clean up its supply chain, or as McDonagh and Braungart might put it, make products that were "less bad": switching to organic cotton or selling fleece jackets made of recycled plastic bottles. The company realized, however, that "less bad" is not good enough; making "greener" products won't cut it if we are all still making and buying more all the time.

In 2011, Patagonia released a now-famous Black Friday ad campaign, "Don't Buy This Jacket." The idea of the campaign was to directly address overconsumption: to come right out and say that most Americans, including Patagonia's own customers, didn't need a lot of the stuff they bought, and that they should buy less of it, full stop. Some critics saw the campaign as hypocritical, since the company was still selling products, and growing. Over the following decade, the company created some real alternatives to selling more and more new stuff, in the form of an increasingly robust repair program (though it doesn't charge for repairs, a big mistake in my mind since revenue from repair is a critical pathway to decoupling a company's growth from the sale of new stuff) and the launch of the Worn Wear program.

Worn Wear seemed to be, at first, mostly a marketing and messaging vehicle. It was also quite literally a vehicle; Patagonia built a funky biodiesel truck to drive around the country, repairing clothes. But eventually the program grew to include a site where customers can actually purchase used Patagonia clothing and gear, recently expanded to include the Recrafted line, with "new" items made from old goods. This is the holy grail of the circular economy: a growing revenue stream from used goods, and eventually hopefully from repair services.

Patagonia does not publish its revenue breakdowns from the Worn Wear site, nor does REI, which has a similar Used Gear site. It's a safe bet that sales from these sites are still minuscule in terms of overall figures for these companies. But they are real, and they make the "Don't Buy This Jacket" campaign less open to critique because they provide an alternative better than just being chilly. To summarize the evolution of Patagonia messaging and corresponding options for customers over the past decades, it goes something like this: First, "Buy jackets that are made better." Then, "Don't buy too many jackets." And finally, "Repair the jacket you have, and if you really need another one, buy it used. As a last resort, buy a well-made new one." That last one is perhaps not very pithy as marketing copy goes, but it pretty much sums up my own shopping philosophy, and it's an important breakthrough that is, slowly, being echoed by more traditional companies.

Patagonia recently adjusted its messaging yet again. In 2018, founder Yvon Chouinard declared in an interview that the mission of the company is no less than "to save the planet." The move reflects a sense of urgency: enough is enough about puffy jackets, this is a crisis bigger than outerwear and we need to act *now*. The new policy also raises the question, how exactly is an outerwear company supposed to save the planet?[7]

Chouinard proposes some specifics on how he plans to support the new policy. Patagonia has, over the years, given millions of dollars to environmental activist groups and community organizations. With the new mission, the company declared its intent to focus that giving on three main areas: policy, public lands, and sustainable agriculture. Chouinard followed this up with a little pithy statement that gave me pause: "Bicycle repair people won't get any more money." Now, we at

Fixup never received any money from Patagonia (and we don't really fix bicycles), but we did receive in-kind support in the form of space when we partnered with New York Patagonia stores to host pop-ups. We set up in their stores, collaborated on outreach, and benefited from the generosity of a much bigger player in the business of saving the world through stuff.

Chouinard's dismissal of the bicycle-repair groups of the world understandably caught my attention. Not because I am worried that we won't benefit from the company's generosity anymore, but because of the implied value statement. Perhaps, in times of crisis, repairing stuff isn't really the right use of energy. It's a thought that has occurred to me several times over the years. Should I in fact be out there on the barricades, dangling from bridges over San Francisco Bay and getting arrested in Washington? (I have done the latter, actually.) Does our stuff really matter at all when over a million species are headed for extinction in the next few decades, when seas are rising, when California is burning, when we are being pummeled by a pandemic—when shit is basically blowing up all around us? In this context, it seems silly to worry about whether your bike or your blender or your chi revitalizer, for god's sake, is working or not. Forget worrying about how Patagonia will save the world—how can one tiny repair shop or one tiny person ever begin to make a difference? That's the elephant sitting with us in this book.

My discomfort with this question is wrapped in my feelings about the title of my 2015 TEDx talk. I stand behind the content of the talk, but the title makes me cringe a bit: "You Can Change the World—with Your Toaster." Titles have always been hard for me. My son Eric—of the late-night bouncing that led to this whole project—was called Baby for a week. I had to pick a title for the talk, though, and (unlike Eric's name) I have disliked it ever since.

Because maybe you can't do shit with your toaster except make toast. Perhaps the title bothers me because, also, it throws the whole endeavor of the past seven years into question. Maybe instead of worrying about toasters and bikes, we should all be like Chouinard and make it our mission—institutional, personal, political, whatever—to save the planet. Actually, I think we should.

But what does that mean we should do? For Chouinard, it seems to mean no longer giving money to bike-repair groups, and instead focusing resources where he thinks they will have the most impact. This seems sensible—in times of crisis, you focus on essential activities. But unfortunately, while we are indeed in a crisis, it is still one that moves slower than the speed of daily human activity, and, at least today as I write this, we still use bikes and blenders and puffy jackets. And Patagonia is presumably still going to continue to sell new jackets (and hopefully more and more used ones). Because that's the elephant in Patagonia's room too. Through it all, as it has spurred changing beliefs about how makers and purveyors of stuff should think about solutions to the climate crisis—through it all it has manufactured and made and sold millions and millions of dollars' worth of stuff. And we have bought it.

It can be discouraging to try to figure out what to do, especially when some are arguing that choices about personal consumption are meaningless at best. David Wallace-Wells dismisses "Western liberals [who] have comforted themselves by contorting their own consumption patterns into performances of moral or environmental purity," while asserting in his climate cri de coeur, *The Uninhabitable Earth* that "I toss out tons of wasted food and hardly ever recycle; I leave my air-conditioning on. . . ." His argument is that individual actions without the "moral multiplier" of political change are not enough. This is true—but it's also not enough.[8]

Certainly, you can't change the world with just your toaster. To save the world, we need to fight for the social and political change that will reshape our economy and facilitate the transition to renewable energy and a circular economy, we need to fairly value and compensate people who make our stuff, we need inclusive and fair governance, and we need to scale solutions quickly, well beyond the scope of any one individual's personal choices or sphere of impact. Given this to-do list, it may seem ludicrous for an outerwear company to make its mission to save the planet, and even more so for one person to buy less stuff and think that it matters. Why not, like Wallace-Wells, just scoff at personally taking the time to recycle or turn off the air conditioner—or fix a toaster?

Because *not* taking these actions—individually—is even more ludicrous; it denies each of us a place in the world. If our actions are part of the problem, then they must be part of the solution. As Jonathan Safran Foer writes:

> The ways we live our lives, the actions we take and don't take, can feed the systemic problems, and they can also change them. . . . Both macro and micro actions have power, and when it comes to mitigating our planetary destruction, it is unethical to dismiss either, or to proclaim that because the large cannot be achieved, the small should not be attempted.[9]

If fixing your toaster will disincline you to vote, or switch to renewable energy, or work to support local repair providers in your community, then by all means, don't fix that toaster. But if you believe, as I do, that our collective actions—our culture—begin in our homes, in our daily lives, and in our hearts, then perhaps you will come to see, as I did, that fixing a damn toaster is just part of a larger fight that we all need to step up and join, each in our own way.

Each of our small choices is the foundation for larger collective shifts: for a movement. Each of us can find ways, in our homes, in our daily lives, and in our hearts, to make changes—and then fight for changes in the world outside our doors. Those of us who work in outerwear need to make outerwear better—to fight with each puffy jacket for the systemic changes in design and production and corporate governance that might indeed help save the world. Those of us who are teachers, or storytellers, or parents, can use those tools to save the world. Whatever your area of expertise or sphere of influence, there is room to make a difference. And if your area of expertise is toasters or bikes—or you simply want to live in a home that aligns with your values—go for it, and use it to fuel your part in the collective fight for change.

As human beings, we will continue to make and use stuff forever (though considerably less of it, I hope). Because, weirdly, in this slow-motion crisis that we are living through, business continues as usual. We will continue to manufacture and use bikes and jackets, and, until we get to the point of suspending normal activities, we had better do it better. And, as I hope you believe after reading this whole book, our bikes and blenders and puffy jackets are intimately linked with who we are, with the way we live, and with the impact we have on the planet and other people around us.

The bottom line is that we don't need more stuff: more Patagonia puffies, more bath mats, more chi revitalizers. We need to see the ones we have in a new light. We need to take care of them, and the people who make—and fix—them. We need to turn our value system upside down in terms of what we think is "good stuff." This sounds like a tall order, but it is possible—one step at a time, one policy at a time, one object at a time.

And in totally rethinking the way we assign value, we might find that we are talking about a lot more than just stuff.

We all have broken stuff.

We have the tools.

Let's fix it.

Acknowledgments

I have spent the past several years of my life on a journey to fix stuff, and understand it—and us—a little bit better in the process. During that time, I taught at Barnard College and designed for theatres across the country. The people with whom I have worked and played in these years were sources of strength, wisdom, and joy, and they helped weave these threads together; I owe them my deepest thanks.

I learned an enormous amount about fixing and so much more from Adam Dowis, whose genius, kindness, and humor inform every page of this book. I am incredibly grateful to Flora Vassar, who devoted her incredible strength, integrity, and ingenuity to the long first year of this project. Along with Adam and Flora, an amazing group of artist-fixers made our shops successful and fun: Simo Peretti, Kim Macron, Michael diPietro, Laura Catignani, Chimmy Gunn, Katie Gordon, Laurel Parrish, Lilla Goettler, Alix Martin, Tom Burgess, Maria Flores, Chris Kavanah, Julie Evanoff, Waverley Engelman, Charis Lam, Stephanie Gonzalez, India Choquette, Monica Wille, and more.

Caitlin Harrington-Smith is an unusually talented young woman whose remarkable good nature and intelligence have been a blessing for the past three years. She helped run repair shops, she was the lead researcher for this book, and she was a brilliant thought partner in creating change. I am very lucky to have had her partnership in writing, investigating, dreaming, and executing so many ideas over the past years.

I am grateful to the team at Island Press for their willingness to take a risk on a designer-fixer-teacher turned writer, especially to my editor, Erin Johnson, who has been steady and supportive throughout. I would never have written this book at all had my agent, Diana Finch, not stopped by the repair shop and asked a simple question, and then helped me turn that idea into a book proposal. Antony Hare provided much more than illustrations; his collaboration and brainstorming were as fantastic as his drawings. I am very grateful for the support of Furthermore, a program of the J. M. Kaplan Fund.

I brought my experiences at the repair shops back to my professional home at Barnard College, where my colleagues helped me connect the dots and turn an unusual project into this book. Kara Feely lent her skills and thoughtfulness, Greg Winkler his steady strength, Alice Reagan her patience and encouragement, Bill Worthen his ability to synthesize ideas, Hana Worthen her thought-provoking insights into topics like posthumanism, and Shayoni Mitra, Gisela Cardenas, and Paige Johnson their support and encouragement. Pam Cobrin and Laurie Postlewaite helped me turn these ideas into a course called Things and Stuff, and Severin Fowles introduced me to a range of wonderful authors and thinkers. Nathalie Molina-Niño was a student-turned-inspiration who helped me realize I had something to say. Barnard is an amazing place where a woman of any age can find her voice, and I would never have been able to embark on such an unusual project without the bravery and out-of-the-box thinking of leaders like Linda Bell, Sian Beilock, Rob Goldberg, Hilary Link, and Debora Spar.

My colleagues and students in Climate Action at Barnard have helped translate some of the ideas in this book into circular programming for our campus community, and have also been both patient and encouraging during the writing and editing process, in particular Leslie Raucher and Lily Farr, but also Fatema Maswood, Maeve Duffy, Batoul Saad, Jade Thompson, Hannah Park, Lhana Ormenyi, Valentina Cartagena, Grace Palmer, Grace Brennan, and more.

I have great admiration for the many brilliant people around the world who are working on repair, including scholars, dreamers, and fixers like Jennifer Russell, Laura Novich, Sahra Svensson, Allison Vicenzi, Linnae Hamilton, Vincent Lai, and more.

My family and friends were willing to help at every step, from watching the boys while I drove vans full of broken stuff around the city to reading drafts of this book. My parents, Peter and Aliette Goldmark, deserve a chapter of thanks to themselves. Priscilla Salant provided encouragement and feedback. Alexis Chiu and Sarah Leibel have known me since I was fourteen years old, and from then until now have shared their love, inspiration, and good edits. Lara Goldmark and Karin Goldmark brought things to be fixed, worked the front desk, watched the kids, and cheered while their little sister tilted against very real windmills.

People across New York and beyond were willing to take a risk on a new idea. At the Greenmarket, Margaret Hoffman, Liz Carrollo, Christina Salvo. At Patagonia, Betsy Pantazelos. Eva Radke at Film Biz Recycling and then ArtCube. Ansley Whipple at the Atlanta BID, Dina Gjertson, the Pawling Farmer's Market, PS 29, Donate NYC, the SWAB, New York Citizen's Committee, and Awesome Without Borders. And of course, our many customers, who joined as cheerful partners in this experiment.

My neighborhood, Inwood, is at the heart of this project and this book. So many friends, neighbors, and community organizations supported our shops: Manny Ramirez at Dichter Pharmacy; the Nagle Avenue Y; UpstART; InwoodKids and Karen Dando; everyone at

Marble Hill Nursery School, including Karen Worchel and David Bleecker-Adams; Bread and Yoga; Annie Nierman and Andy Beck; Alice Reagan and Shane LeClair; Margaret Blachly and Catlin Preston; and our neighbors in the building, who brought their broken stuff and put up with the occasional mess, especially Martha Langmuir, Martha Alexander, and Osvaldo Torres.

Luke and Eric were cheerful, loving, and always willing to help fix (and sometimes break) things with us.

In work and life and play, from design to theatre to Barnard to child-rearing to getting up at 5 a.m. and driving repair vans to fixing almost everything to the last little line edits, my partner has been my husband and colleague, Michael Banta—for whom I am more grateful than any words could convey. And there, at least, is one thing that doesn't need fixing.

Notes

Author's Note

1. Austin Ivereigh, "Pope Francis Says Pandemic Can Be a 'Place of Conversion,'" *The Tablet,* April 8, 2020, https://www.thetablet.co.uk/features /2/17845/pope-francis-says-pandemic-can-be-a-place-of-conversion.

Introduction: Broken Sleep

1. Diana Ivanova et al., "Environmental Impact Assessment of Household Consumption," *Journal of Industrial Ecology* 20, no. 3 (December 2015), https://doi.org/10.1111/jiec.12371; "CO_2 Emissions (Metric Tons per Capita)," The World Bank, accessed February 20, 2020, https://data .worldbank.org/indicator/EN.ATM.CO2E.PC.

   Even more of a wake-up call for those who live in the United States— these global figures can be deceiving, as impacts (and benefits) are not shared equally around the world. The United States is among the biggest emitters of GHG, largely because of the lifestyle of our citizens. Globally, in 2014, average per capita CO_2 emissions were 4.9 metric tons while in the United States, the average was 16.5 metric tons per person.

2. "Opportunities to Reduce Greenhouse Gas Emissions through Materials and Land Management Practices," US Environmental Protection Agency, September 2009, https://19january2017snapshot.epa.gov/sites/production /files/2016–08/documents/ghg-land-materials-management.pdf.

3. "How Big Is the Great Pacific Garbage Patch? Science vs. Myth," National

Oceanic and Atmospheric Administration, accessed February 9, 2020, https://response.restoration.noaa.gov/about/media/how-big-great-pacific -garbage-patch-science-vs-myth.html; University of California, Irvine, "Manufacturing, Global Trade Impair Health of People with No Stake in Either: Expert Helps Map Migration of Air Pollution Risk to Regions Far from Factories," *ScienceDaily*, March 17, 2020, https://www.sciencedaily .com/releases/2017/03/170329145728.htm; "The Rana Plaza Accident and Its Aftermath," International Labour Organization, accessed February 9 2020, https://www.ilo.org/global/topics/geip/WCMS_614394/lang—en /index.htm; Leonard, "Facts from *The Story of Stuff*," accessed February 9, 2020, https://storyofstuff.org/wp-content/uploads/movies/scripts/Storyof Stuff_FactSheet.pdf.

4. "Table 2.4.5. Personal Consumption Expenditures by Type of Product: Annual," Federal Reserve Bank of St. Louis, accessed February 9, 2020, https://fred.stlouisfed.org/release/tables?eid=44183&rid=53.

5. Samantha Putt del Pino et al., "Elephant in the Boardroom: Why Unchecked Consumption Is Not an Option in Tomorrow's Markets" (World Resources Institute, 2017).

6. "Completing the Picture: How the Circular Economy Tackles Climate Change," Ellen MacArthur Foundation, September 26, 2019, https:// www.ellenmacarthurfoundation.org/publications/completing-the-picture -climate-change.

7. Pollan, "Unhappy Meals," *New York Times*, January 28, 2007, https:// www.nytimes.com/2007/01/28/magazine/28nutritionism.t.html.

8. For more on learning from the past, see the discussion in Chapter 7 on David Sax's concept of "rearview innovation."

Chapter 1. Our Long and Tangled Story of Stuff

1. "Rationality is logical coherence—reasonable or not. Econs are rational by this definition, but there is overwhelming evidence that Humans cannot be. . . . The definition of rationality as coherence is impossibly restrictive; it demands adherence to rules of logic that a finite mind is not able to implement." Daniel Kahneman, *Thinking, Fast and Slow* (New York: Farrar, Straus and Giroux, 2011), 411.

2. Hodder, *Where Are We Heading? The Evolution of Humans and Things* (New Haven, CT: Yale University Press, 2018), xii.

3. Hodder, *Where Are We Heading?*, 8.

4. Miller, *Stuff* (Cambridge, UK: Polity Press, 2010), 5.

5. Brown, *Things* (Chicago: University of Chicago Press, 2004), 4.

6. Miller, *Stuff*, 12.

Chapter 2. The Good, the Bad, and the Ugly Truth about How Stuff Got That Way

1. "iPad 4 Wi-Fi Repair," iFixit, accessed February 9, 2020, https://www.ifixit.com/Device/iPad_4_Wi-Fi.

2. "iPad 7 Repair," iFixit, accessed February 9, 2020, https://www.ifixit.com/Device/iPad_7.

3. Dami Lee, "Apple Says There Are 1.4 Billion Active Apple Devices," *The Verge*, January 29, 2019, https://www.theverge.com/2019/1/29/18202736/apple-devices-ios-earnings-q1–2019.

4. C. P. Baldé et al., "The Global E-waste Monitor 2017," (Bonn/Geneva/Vienna: United Nations University, International Telecommunication Union & International Solid Waste Association, 2017), https://collections.unu.edu/eserv/UNU: 6341/Global-E-waste_Monitor_2017__electronic_single_pages_.pdf.

5. Antonio Villas-Boas, "Apple's New $1,100 iPhone 11 Pro Max Weighs a Whopping Half a Pound, Making It the Heaviest iPhone Ever," *Business Insider*, September 12, 2019, https://www.businessinsider.com/apple-iphone-11-pro-max-weight-half-pound-heaviest-iphone-2019–9.

6. "Apple Expands Global Recycling Programs," Apple, April 18, 2019, https://www.apple.com/newsroom/2019/04/apple-expands-global-recycling-programs/.

7. C. P. Baldé et al., "The Global E-waste Monitor 2014," (Bonn, Germany: United Nations University, IAS SCYCLE, 2014), http: //i.unu.edu/media/ias.unu.edu-en/news/7916/Global-E-waste-Monitor-2014-small.pdf.

8. William McDonough and Michael Braungart, *Cradle to Cradle: Remaking the Way We Make Things* (New York: North Point Press, 2002), 28.

9. Leonard, "Facts from *The Story of Stuff*" (see Intro., n. 6).

10. "2019 Environmental Responsibility Report," Apple, accessed February 20, 2020, https://www.apple.com/environment/pdf/Apple_Environmental_Responsibility_Report_2019.pdf.

11. Brian Merchant, "Op-Ed: Were the Raw Materials in Your iPhone Mined by Children in Inhumane Conditions?" *Los Angeles Times*, July 23, 2017, https://www.latimes.com/opinion/op-ed/la-oe-merchant-iphone-supply chain-20170723-story.html.

12. London, "Ending the Depression through Planned Obsolescence," 1932, 2. For an excellent and thorough account of the various forms of obsolescence—planned, technological, psychological—read Giles Slade's *Made to Break: Technology and Obsolescence in America*.

13. Bill Chappell, "Apple Says It Slows Older iPhones to Save Their Battery Life," NPR, December 21, 2017, https://www.npr.org/sections/thetwo -way/2017/12/21/572538593/apple-says-it-slows-older-iphones-to-save -their-battery-life.

14. Chris Welch, "Apple Explains Why iPhones Now Show an Ominous Warning after 'Unauthorized' Battery Replacements," *The Verge*, August 14, 2019, https://www.theverge.com/2019/8/14/20805744/apple-iphone -battery-replacements-ios-safety-statement-unauthorized.

15. Slade, *Made to Break*, 157.

16. Brent Schlender and Rick Tetzeli, *Becoming Steve Jobs: The Evolution of a Reckless Upstart into a Visionary Leader* (New York: Crown Business, 2015), 454.

17. "Fairphone 3 Teardown," iFixit, accessed February 9, 2020, https://www .ifixit.com/Teardown/Fairphone+3+Teardown/125573.

18. "Nespresso CitiZ Teardown," iFixit, accessed February 9, 2020, https:// www.ifixit.com/Teardown/Nespresso+CitiZ+Teardown/42890.

19. "Design choices aren't the only way manufacturers prevent repair. Many companies, for example, choose not to offer official replacement parts to individuals or repair techs. 'We're used to being able to buy replacement parts for our cars and appliances, but that's often not the case with your smartphone or laptop,' Suovanen, iFixit engineer says. And when manufacturers refuse to sell Original Equipment Manufacturer (OEM) parts, repair shops and users have to turn to third-party components instead, which can be problematic." Whitson Gordon, "The Most Common Ways Manufacturers Prevent You from Repairing Your Devices," iFixit, April 17, 2019, https://www.ifixit.com/News/the-most-common-ways-manu facturers-prevent-you-from-repairing-your-devices.

20. Sophia Yan, "'Made in China' Isn't So Cheap Anymore, and That Could

Spell Headache for Beijing," CNBC, February 27, 2017, https: //www
.cnbc.com/2017/02/27/chinese-wages-rise-made-in-china-isnt-so-cheap
-anymore.html.

21. Lucie Venard, "Get Paid to Fix Your Broken Things—New Swedish Tax
Breaks Support Repair," Medium.com, March 1, 2017, https://medium
.com/@greenxeurope/getting-paid-to-fix-your-broken-things-new-swedish
-tax-breaks-support-repair-ff67c016c211.

22. "A Nightmare for Workers: Appalling Conditions in Toy Factories Persist,"
China Labor Watch, December 6, 2018, http://www.chinalaborwatch.org
/report/138.

Part II. Not Too Much

1. Worldlink Staff, "Nourish: Food + Community to Air on PBS: What's
the Story of Your Food?," *Nourish Life*, September 21, 2010, https://www
.nourishlife.org/about/press-room/press-releases/nourish-on-pbs/.

Chapter 3. Our Stuff, Our Selves

1. Frost, "Hoarding: Making Disorder an Official Disorder," *Insight Smith
College*, September 14, 2012, https: //www.smith.edu/insight/stories/dis
order.php.

2. "Diagnosing Hoarding Disorder," International OCD Foundation,
accessed February 9, 2020, https://hoarding.iocdf.org/professionals/diag
nosing?hoarding-disorder/.

3. "IBISWorld Industry Report 53113," IBISWorld, accessed February 9,
2020, https://clients1.ibisworld.com/reports/us/industry/default.aspx?ent
id=1351.

4. In *Looking at Shakespeare*, Dennis Kennedy writes that design can be used
"not only to establish environment and atmosphere but also to create a
complicated theatrical signifier of its thematic approach . . . most productions use stage and costume design to comment on the play, as a guide
to the interpretive treatment." Kennedy, *Looking at Shakespeare: A Visual
History of Twentieth-Century Performance* (Cambridge: Cambridge University Press, 1993), 3.

5. "Table 2.4.5. Personal Consumption Expenditures by Type of Product:
Annual," Federal Reserve Bank of St. Louis, accessed February 9, 2020,
https://fred.stlouisfed.org/release/tables?eid=44183&rid=53. For the
purposes of this book, we calculate our "stuff budget" based on the FRED

tables for Personal Consumption Expenditures. We have removed motor vehicles and added clothing (which is counted by FRED as "nondurable"), for a total of approximately $4,000 per year per American individual, or $11,000 per household. Overall, Americans spend more than $4 trillion per year on the "stuff" described in this book—home goods, clothing, appliances, and so forth.

6. Emma Johnson, "The Real Cost of Your Shopping Habits," *Forbes*, January 15, 2015, https://www.forbes.com/sites/emmajohnson/2015/01/15/the-real-cost-of-your-shopping-habits/#4fc67cb61452.

7. Ray Smith, "A Closet Filled with Regrets," *Wall Street Journal*, April 17, 2013, https://www.wsj.com/articles/SB10001424127887324240804578415002232186418.

8. Ross, *Clothing: A Global History* (Cambridge, UK: Polity Press, 2008), 7.

9. Ross, 7.

10. Pollan, *The Omnivore's Dilemma: A Natural History of Four Meals* (New York: Penguin Press, 2006), 302.

11. "An Epidemic of Obesity: U.S. Obesity Trends," Harvard T. H. Chan School of Public Health, accessed February 9, 2020, https://www.hsph.harvard.edu/nutritionsource/an-epidemic-of-obesity/. See also "Why Are Americans Obese?" Public Health, accessed February 9, 2020, https://www.publichealth.org/public-awareness/obesity/.

12. Pollan, *In Defense of Food: An Eater's Manifesto* (New York: Penguin Press, 2008), 89. Pollan compares this Western diet to "traditional diets," and, in assessing the health impacts of the former, draws on Walter C. Willett, "The Pursuit of Optimal Diets: A Progress Report."

13. "US Food System," University of Michigan, accessed February 9, 2020, http://css.umich.edu/factsheets/us-food-system-factsheet.

Chapter 4. The Global Conspiracy to Clutter Your Home

1. Leonard provides a thorough explanation of externalities:

Earth Economics (eartheconomics.org) defines an externality as "Externality: An unintended and uncompensated loss or gain in the welfare of one party resulting from an activity of another party." Another way to explain this is that there are many real costs of producing things (like using water, dumping waste, contributing to climate change, paying sick worker's medical care) which are incurred by producing things, but are ignored by the company owners. Since the company owners don't pay for these real costs, but shift them onto the public and the environment, they are said to 'externalize' them which means making someone else pay for them. That is what I mean when I say that the prices of many goods don't reflect the true cost of making the things. Someone else is paying for the doctors' bills, the longer hike to get water after local water is polluted or gone, the impacts of climate change, the cost of the asthma inhaler and more costs incurred from the extraction, production, distribution and disposal of stuff.

Annie Leonard, "Story of Stuff, Referenced and Annotated Script," The Story of Stuff Project, 7, https://www.storyofstuff.org/wp-content /uploads/2020/01/StoryofStuff_AnnotatedScript.pdf.

2. "Inter IKEA Group Financial Summary FY18," Yearly Summary, IKEA, https://preview.thenewsmarket.com/Previews/IKEA/DocumentAssets /525318.pdf; Paul Emrath, "Spaces in New Homes," National Associa- tion of Home Builders, March 14, 2019, https://www.nahb.org/News -and-Economics/Housing-Economics/Special-Studies/Spaces-in-New -Homes; Liam O'Connell, "Number of Employees of the IKEA Group Worldwide from 2017 to 2019" (October 15, 2019), distributed by Statista, https://www.statista.com/statistics/241825/number-of-employ ees-of-the-ikea-group-worldwide-by-function/; "IKEA Helps Customers Find Their Way with Indoor Google Maps," Case Studies, Google Maps, last modified June 22, 2012, https://static.googleusercontent.com /media/maps.google.com/en//help/maps/indoormaps/assets/casestudies /ikea-cs-20120622.pdf; "IKEA Group FY14 Yearly Summary," Yearly Summary, IKEA, last modified August 31, 2014, https://www.ikea.com /ms/en_US/pdf/yearly_summary/ikea-group-yearly-summary-fy14.pdf; Ryan Gorman, "IKEA Uses a Staggering 1% of the World's Wood Every Year," *Daily Mail*, July 5, 2013, https://www.dailymail.co.uk/news/article -2357216/IKEA-uses-staggering-1-worlds-wood-year.html; Robert Galavan, John Murray, and Costas Marksides, *Strategy, Innovation, and Change: Challenges for Management* (Oxford: Oxford University Press, 2008).

3. Ingvar Kamprad and Bertil Torekull, *Leading by Design: The Ikea Story* (New York: HarperBusiness, 1999), 50.

4. Robert Galavan, John Murray, and Costas Marksides, *Strategy, Innovation, and Change: Challenges for Management* (Oxford: Oxford University Press, 2008), 151.

5. David Lester, ed., *How They Started Global Brands: How 21 Good Ideas Became Great Global Businesses* (Richmond: Crimson, 2008), 130.

6. "Durable Goods: Product-Specific Data," US Environmental Protection Agency, accessed February 20, 2020, https://www.epa.gov/facts-and -figures-about-materials-waste-and-recycling/durable-goods-product -specific-data.

7. Lauren Collins, "House Perfect: Is the IKEA Ethos Comfy or Creepy?" *New Yorker*, October 3, 2011, https://www.newyorker.com/magazine /2011/10/03/house-perfect.

8. Naresh Ramchandani, "Naresh Ramchandani: The Power of Grace and Words," uploaded December 16, 2016, YouTube video, 0:23, https:// www.youtube.com/watch? v=hj22zTIoRuA.

9. Nick Paumgarten, "Patagonia's Philosopher-King," *New Yorker*, September 12, 2016.

10. "IKEA Highlights 2019," IKEA Facts and Figures, IKEA, accessed February 19, 2020, https://about.ikea.com/en/organisation/ikea-facts-and -figures/ikea-highlights-2019; "Inter IKEA Group Financial Summary FY17," IKEA, accessed February 19, 2020, https://preview.thenewsmarket .com/Previews/IKEA/DocumentAssets/493700.pdf.

11. First Research, "Used Merchandise Stores Industry Profile," Dun & Brad-street, accessed February 11, 2020, http://www.firstresearch.com/industry -research/Used-Merchandise-Stores.html.

12. "The Circular Economy Could Unlock $4.5 Trillion of Economic Growth, Finds New Book by Accenture," Accenture, September 28, 2015, https:// newsroom.accenture.com/news/the-circular-economy-could-unlock-4-5 -trillion-of-economic-growth-finds-new-book-by-accenture.htm.

Part III. Mostly Reclaimed

1. Laurie Sullivan, "Success of YouTube Unboxing and Store Haul Videos a Phenomenon," MediaPost, December 13, 2018, https://www.mediapost .com/publications/article/329245/success-of-youtube-unboxing-and-store -haul-videos.html.

2. "Why Are Americans Obese?," PublicHealth (see chap. 3, n. 11).

Chapter 5. Getting Good at Getting Used

1. First Research, "Used Merchandise Stores Industry Profile," Dun &

Bradstreet, accessed February 11, 2020, http://www.firstresearch.com
/industry-research/Used-Merchandise-Stores.html.

2. Interestingly, we did not advertise the swap only to women, and the language for the event was not obviously gendered, but only women signed
up.

3. Erica van Herpen and Ilona de Hooge explain: "Consumers thus have
an aversion to throwing away unused utility, indicated by feelings of discomfort, whereas transferring utility to another consumer does not lead
to similar feelings of discomfort." Van Herpen and de Hooge, "When
Product Attitudes Go to Waste: Wasting Products with Remaining Utility
Decreases Consumers' Product Attitudes," *Journal of Cleaner Production*
210 (February 2019): 410–18, https://doi.org/10.1016/j.jclepro.2018
.10.331; Remi Trudel, Jennifer J. Argo, Matthew D. Meng, "The Recycled Self: Consumers' Disposal Decisions of Identity-Linked Products,"
Journal of Consumer Research 43, no. 2 (August 2016): 246–64, https://
doi.org/10.1093/jcr/ucw014.

4. Henry David Thoreau, *Walden; or, Life in the Woods* (London: J. M.
Dent, 1908), 163.

5. "Calculadora CO_2," Asociación Española de Recuperadores de Economía
Social y Solidaria, accessed February 11, 2020, http://reutilizayevitaco2
.aeress.org; "Most Profitable Pieces of Merchandise in the U.S. 2012, by
Average Retail Price," Statista, accessed February 19, 2020, https://www
.statista.com/statistics/241289/most-profitable-pieces-of-merchandise-in
-the-us-by-average-retail-price/; "Apparel Worldwide," Statista, accessed
February 19, 2020, https://www.statista.com/outlook/90040300/100
/apparel/worldwide.

Big caveat here—a lot of these carbon calculations are notoriously
fuzzy. It's very hard to actually calculate the impact of any particular item,
and even more difficult to estimate the emissions *avoided* through reuse.
But several calculators exist, and they all indicate that the savings from
reuse are significant when considered at scale. This estimate was based
on data from a CO_2 calculator published by the Asociación Española de
Recuperadores de Economía Social y Solidaria.

Check out the Reuse Network's CO_2 impact calculator for additional
estimations of carbon savings for reuse. For estimations of emissions from
new manufacturing, https://www.carbonfootprint.com has a calculator
for "secondary" purchases.

In our shirt example, we assume $22,971 million (US$12,992M for women, US$6,862M for men, and US$3,117M for children) in annual spending on shirts in the United States. If we then suppose the average US shirt retail price is $15, then $1,531 million shirts are sold annually in the States. If everyone living in America bought used shirts instead of new for a year, and we assume one used shirt corresponds to 2.5 kg CO_2e prevented, that would save 3,828,500 tons CO_2e from entering the atmosphere.

6. Suzy Strutner, "Here's What Goodwill Actually Does with Your Donated Clothes," *HuffPost*, last modified April 12, 2019, https://www.huffpost .com/entry/what-does-goodwill-do-with-your-clothes_n_57e06b96e4b00 71a6e092352? section; Department of Economic and Social Affairs, *International Trade Statistics Yearbook Volume II 2017* (New York: United Nations, 2019), 77, https://comtrade.un.org/pb/downloads/2017/VolII 2017.pdf; "A World Hungry for Used Clothing," Planetaid, accessed February 19, 2020, https://www.planetaid.org/our-work/recycling/global -trade; "Textiles: Material-Specific Data," US Environmental Protection Agency, accessed February 19, 2020, https://www.epa.gov/facts-and-figures -about-materials-waste-and-recycling/textiles-material-specific-data.

7. "Which of These Articles Have You Bought Second Hand in the Past 12 Months (No Matter If Online or in Person)?" Statista Global Consumer Survey 2019, accessed February 19, 2020, https://www.statista.com /forecasts/997103/second-hand-purchases-by-category-in-the-us.

8. Anna-Adelaine Hansson and Evgenia Morozov, "Driving Forces towards Shopping for Second-Hand Clothing," Lund University, May 2016, https://pdfs.semanticscholar.org/0f58/4c06f74741059dd91f892793fc7 5bbb1e145.pdf; Fabio Shimabukuro Sandes and Julio César Leandro, "Exploring the Motivations and Barriers for Second Hand Product Consumption," Escola de Administração de Empresas de São Paulo, accessed February 19, 2020, http://bibliotecadigital.fgv.br/ocs/index.php/clav/clav 2016/paper/view/5854.

9. "National Thrift Store Day: August 17, 2018," US Census Bureau, last modified August 9, 2018, https://www.census.gov/newsroom/stories/2018 /thrift-store.html; "Annual Report 2018," NYC Department of Sanitation, accessed February 19, 2020, https://dsnydonate.cityofnewyork.us /wp-content/uploads/2018/09/2018-donateNYC-AnnualReport-FINAL .pdf.

10. "The Future of Shopping Centers," A. T. Kearney, accessed February 19,

2020, https://www.kearney.com/documents/20152/986752/The+Future
+of+Shopping+Centers.pdf/6455ae6f-f430–2fe7–2856-ef671153d29a.

11. Fung Global Retail & Technology, "Fast Fashion Speeding toward Ultra-fast Fashion," May 19, 2017, https://coresight.com/wp-content/uploads
/2017/05/Fast-Fashion-Speeding-Toward-Ultrafast-Fashion-May-19
_2017. pdf.

12. Lauren Thomas, "Poshmark Took on Secondhand Apparel, Now It's Get-ting into Home Décor," CNBC, June 11, 2019, https://www.cnbc.com
/2019/06/11/retail-resell-site-poshmark-is-getting-into-home-decor.html.

13. "A New Textiles Economy: Redesigning Fashion's Future," Ellen MacAr-thur Foundation, last modified December 1, 2017, https://www.ellenmac
arthurfoundation.org/assets/downloads/publications/A-New-Textiles-Econ
omy_Summary-of-Findings_Updated_1–12–17. pdf.

14. "ThredUP 2019 Resale Report," GlobalData, accessed February 19,
2020, https://www.thredup.com/resale.

15. Laurel Thatcher Ulrich, "Hannah Barnard's Cupboard," chap. 3 in *The
Age of Homespun: Objects and Stories in the Creation of an American Myth*
(New York: Random House, 2001).

As Ulrich explains, women especially were handed down these types
of goods, since they often were not able to inherit land or houses. More
detail on the historically high value of textiles can be found in the fasci-nating research in *Women's Work: The First 20,000 Years: Women, Cloth,
and Society in Early Times* by Elizabeth Wayland Barber.

Part IV: Care for It

1. Suzan-Lori Parks, *The America Play and Other Works* (New York: Theatre
Communications Group, 1995), 9.

Chapter 6. Making and Mending in America

1. Grey, *Riders of the Purple Sage* (New York: Grosset & Dunlap, 1912), 15.

2. For a detailed account of the role of African American quilting in shap-ing American society, Kyra E. Hicks's *Black Threads* is an indispensable
resource.

3. Ulrich, *Age of Homespun*, 14–16 (see chap. 5, n. 17).

4. "Employment by Industry, 1910 and 2015," US Bureau of Labor Statis-tics, March 3, 2016, https://www.bls.gov/opub/ted/2016/employment-by
-industry-1910-and-2015.htm.

5. Kimberly Amadeo, "US Manufacturing Statistics and Outlook," The Balance, October 22, 2019, https://www.thebalance.com/u-s-manufactur ing-what-it-is-statistics-and-outlook-3305575.

6. Milkman, *Farewell to the Factory: Auto Workers in the Late Twentieth Century* (Berkeley: University of California Press, 1997).

7. Emerson, *Man the Reformer: A Lecture, Etc.* (Manchester: Abel Heywood, 1843), 5.

8. Strasser, *Waste and Want: A Social History of Trash* (New York: Metropolitan Books, 1999), 10.

Chapter 7. The Fixers

1. Beilock, *How the Body Knows Its Mind: The Surprising Power of the Physical Environment to Influence How You Think and Feel* (New York: Atria Books, 2017), 7. Beilock is also the president of Barnard College, where I teach.

2. Beilock, *How the Body Knows*, 49.

3. Anderson, *Makers: The New Industrial Revolution* (New York: Crown Business, 2014), 22.

4. *Adweek* has a useful summary of the maker movement:

   The maker movement, as we know, is the umbrella term for independent inventors, designers and tinkerers. A convergence of computer hackers and traditional artisans, the niche is established enough to have its own magazine, *Make*, as well as hands-on Maker Faires that are catnip for DIYers who used to toil in solitude. Makers tap into an American admiration for self-reliance and combine that with open-source learning, contemporary design and powerful personal technology like 3-D printers. The creations, born in cluttered local workshops and bedroom offices, stir the imaginations of consumers numbed by generic, mass-produced, made-in-China merchandise.

   Joan Voight, "Which Big Brands Are Courting the Maker Movement, and Why," *Adweek*, March 17, 2014, http://www.adweek.com/news /advertising-branding/which-big-brands-are-courting-maker-movement -and-why-156315.

5. Anderson, *Makers*, 16.

6. David Sax, "End the Innovation Obsession," *New York Times*, December 7, 2018.

Chapter 8. God and Stuff

1. Matthew 6:19–21, *ESV Study Bible: English Standard Version* (Wheaton, IL: Crossway Bibles, 2016).

2. White, "The Historical Roots of Our Ecological Crisis," *Science* 155, no. 3767 (March 1967): 1203–07, https://science.sciencemag.org/content /155/3767/1203.

3. Swimme and Tucker, *Journey of the Universe* (New Haven, CT: Yale University Press, 2011), 103; "Our History," Journey of the Universe, accessed February 21, 2020, https://www.journeyoftheuniverse.org/about. Swimme is an evolutionary cosmologist and professor at the California Institute of Integral Studies in San Francisco. Tucker teaches at the Yale School of Forestry and Environmental Studies and Yale Divinity School and cofounded the Yale Forum on Religion and Ecology. Their work, *Journey of the Universe*, was inspired by Thomas Berry and the idea that "we needed to bring science and humanities together in an integrated cosmology that would guide humans into the next period of human-Earth relations."

4. For a thorough account of the humanistic worldview and how it has shaped our lives, check out Yuval Noah Harari's *Sapiens: A Brief History of Humankind.* Go even further and explore how a limited definition of "human" can run out of steam in more ways than one in *The Post Human*, by Rosi Braidotti.

5. Locke, *The Second Treatise of Civil Government and A Letter Concerning Toleration* (Oxford, UK: B. Blackwell, 1948).

6. Vine Deloria, Jr., "Kinship with the World," in *Spirit and Reason: The Vine Deloria, Jr. Reader*, ed. Samuel Scinta, Kristen Foehner, and Barbara Deloria (Golden, Colorado: Fulcrum Publishing, 1999), 223–29.

7. "Encyclical Letter *Laudato Si'* of the Holy Father Francis on Care for Our Common Home," The Vatican, accessed February 20, 2020, http://www .vatican.va/content/francesco/en/encyclicals/documents/papa-francesco _20150524_enciclica-laudato-si.html.

8. "*Laudato Si'.*"

9. Dwivedi, "Dharmic Ecology," in *Hinduism and Ecology: The Intersection of Earth, Sky, and Water*, ed. Christopher Chapple and Mary Evelyn Tucker (Cambridge, MA: Harvard University Press and the Center for the Study of World Religions: 2000), 3–22.

10. M. N. Dutta, *Mahabharata* (Delhi: Parimal Publications, 1988), chapter 182, verses 14–19.

11. "Gaia hypothesis," Encyclopaedia Britannica, accessed February 20, 2020, https://www.britannica.com/science/Gaia-hypothesis. As more proof of the multiplicity of ways to understand the earth, Amla mentioned the goddess Prithvi to me, who in Hinduism and some forms of Buddhism is a "Mother Earth" goddess. Gaia, in the Greek tradition, is also Mother Earth, and later inspired the Gaia hypothesis, which posits that the earth itself is a "coordinated whole," like a living being. And numerous Indigenous traditions treat the earth as a being that deserves care and respect.

12. "United States Average Hourly Wages," Trading Economics, accessed February 20, 2020, https://tradingeconomics.com/united-states/wages; "Average Caregiver Hourly Pay," PayScale, accessed February 20, 2020, https://www.payscale.com/research/US/Job=Caregiver/Hourly_Rate.

13. Ukeles, "Manifesto for Maintenance Art, 1969!," Queens Museum, April 2016, https://queensmuseum.org/wp-content/uploads/2016/04/Ukeles-Manifesto-for-Maintenance-Art-1969.pdf.

14. "Mierle Laderman Ukeles: Maintenance Art," Queens Museum, September, 18, 2016, https://queensmuseum.org/wp-content/uploads/2016/12/Mierle% 20Laderman% 20Ukeles_Maintenance% 20Art_Brochure.pdf.

15. Tony Watling, *Ecological Imaginations in the World Religions: An Ethnographic Analysis* (New York: Continuum, 2012), 85–87; Roger S. Gottlieb, *The Oxford Handbook of Religion and Ecology* (Oxford: Oxford University Press, 2010), 227.

16. Watling, *Ecological Imaginations*.

17. Kennedy, *Looking at Shakespeare* (see chap. 3, n. 4). Dennis Kennedy argues that design elements onstage create layers of meaning, independent of, in concert with, and sometimes in contrast to the meaning of the written or spoken words. This "scenography," or scenic writing, is one of the strongest and clearest ways to help the audience understand the rules of the imaginary world they are experiencing. Design, as thematic signifiers, can be clues or guidelines that help us grasp the logic of the overall production.

18. Pollan, *How to Change Your Mind: What the New Science of Psychedelics Teaches Us about Consciousness, Dying, Addiction, Depression, and Transcendence* (New York: Penguin Books, 2019), 413.

19. Pollan, *How to Change Your Mind*, 128.

Chapter 9. From Cradle to Grave

1. "Statement on the Purpose of a Corporation," Business Roundtable, last modified September 6, 2019, https://opportunity.businessroundtable.org /wp-content/uploads/2019/09/BRT-Statement-on-the-Purpose-of-a-Cor poration-with-Signatures-1. pdf.

2. "Thrift Stores Say They're Swamped with Donations after 'Tidying Up with Marie Kondo,'" interview by Audie Cornish, *All Things Considered*, NPR, January 21, 2019, audio, https://www.npr.org/2019/01/21/68725 5642/thrift-stores-say-theyre-swamped-with-donations-after-tidying-up -with-marie-kond; Mary Hanbury, "We Went to a Goodwill Store and Saw How It's 'Overrun' with Stuff Millennials and Gen Xers Refuse to Take from Their Parents," *Business Insider*, June 8, 2018, https://www .businessinsider.com/millennials-fill-goodwill-stores-with-donations-photos -2018–2.

3. Don Fullerton and Thomas Kinnaman, "Household Responses for Pricing Garbage by the Bag," *American Economic Review* 86, no. 4 (1996): 971– 84, https://doi.org/https://www.researchgate.net/publication/4732858 _Household_Responses_to_Pricing_Garbage_by_the_Bag; Elisabeth Rosenthal, "By 'Bagging It,' Ireland Rids Itself of a Plastic Nuisance," *New Yorker*, January 21, 2008, https://www.nytimes.com/2008/01/31 /world/europe/31iht-bags.4.9650382.html; Douglas Broom, "South Korea Once Recycled 2% of Its Food Waste. Now It Recycles 95%," World Economic Forum, April 12, 2019 https://www.weforum.org /agenda/2019/04/south-korea-recycling-food-waste/; "Bulk Pickup," Republic Services, accessed February 21, 2020, http://local.republicser vices.com/site/Lafayette-co/Documents/bulk-pick-up.pdf; Jeremy Anderberg, "How to Get Rid of Old Furniture and Large Items of Trash," *Art of Manliness*, March 17, 2018, https://www.artofmanliness.com/articles /how-to-dispose-of-old-furniture-and-remove-other-large-items-of-trash/.

4. Curb Alert NYC (@curbalertnyc), Instagram account, accessed February, 21, 2020, https://www.instagram.com/curbalertnyc/?hl=en.

5. "Electronics Recycling," Services, ERI, accessed February 21, 2020, https://eridirect.com/services/electronics-recycling-ewaste/.

6. "Electronic Recycling," ERI.

7. Jim Puckett, "Secret Tracking Project Finds That Your Old Electronic Waste Gets Exported to Developing Countries," Basel Action Network, September 15, 2016, https://www.ban.org/news/2016/9/15/secret-tracking

-project-finds-that-your-old-electronic-waste-gets-exported-to-developing
-countries.

8. "Eco-Friendly Junk Removal," Why Us, The Junkluggers, accessed February 21, 2020, https://www.junkluggers.com/about-us/why-us/eco-friendly
-junk-removal.html.

9. Jake Halpern, "The Big Business of Scavenging in Postindustrial America," *New York Times*, August 22, 2019, https://www.nytimes.com/2019
/08/21/magazine/the-big-business-of-scavenging-in-postindustrial-amer
ica.html.

Conclusion: Fight for It

1. Kolbert, *The Sixth Extinction: An Unnatural History* (London: Blooms-
bury, 2014), 17.

2. Yinon M. Bar-On, Rob Phillips, and Ron Milo, "The Biomass Distribution on Earth," *Proceedings of the National Academy of Sciences* 115, no. 25
(June 2018): 6506–11, https://www.pnas.org/content/115/25/6506.

3. "Today, the biomass of humans ($\approx$0.06 Gt C; *SI Appendix*, Table S9) and
the biomass of livestock ($\approx$0.1 Gt C, dominated by cattle and pigs; *SI
Appendix*, Table S10) far surpass that of wild mammals, which has a mass
of $\approx$0.007 Gt C (*SI Appendix*, Table S11)." Bar-On, Phillips, and Milo,
"The Biomass Distribution on Earth."

4. "Trends in Global Export Volume of Trade in Goods from 1950 to
2018," Statista, accessed February 19, 2020, https://www.statista.com
/statistics/264682/worldwide-export-volume-in-the-trade-since-1950/.

5. MacGregor, *A History of the World in 100 Objects* (New York: Viking
Penguin, 2011), 19–25.

6. Yvon Chouinard and Vincent Stanley, *The Responsible Company: What
We've Learned from Patagonia's First 40 Years* (Ventura, CA: Patagonia
Books, 2012).

7. Jeff Beer, "Exclusive: 'Patagonia Is in Business to Save Our Home Planet,'"
Fast Company, December 13, 2018, https://www.fastcompany.com
/90280950/exclusive-patagonia-is-in-business-to-save-our-home-planet.

8. Wallace-Wells, *The Uninhabitable Earth: A Story of the Future* (London:
Allen Lane, 2019), 33.

9. Foer, *We Are the Weather: Saving the Planet Begins at Breakfast* (New York:
Farrar, Straus and Giroux, 2019), 200.

About the Author

Sandra Goldmark is an assistant professor of Professional Practice in Theatre at Barnard College, where she serves as the Director for Sustainability and Climate Action, leading a 360-degree approach to integrate climate action into academics, finance and governance, and campus operations and culture. In 2013, Sandra founded Fixup (formerly Pop Up Repair), to develop circular economy solutions to overconsumption and waste. Fixup has operated more than a dozen pop-up repair shops, organized numerous educational events, and repaired thousands of broken items.

Prior to founding Fixup and tackling climate action at Barnard, Sandra designed scenery for theatres in New York and around the country. Together with colleagues in the Barnard College Theatre Department, she developed and championed a circular design and production initiative and tool kit for theatres.

Sandra lives in New York with her husband, Michael, and their two children.